CIVILIZATION
IN
ANCIENT INDIA

CIVILIZATION
IN
ANCIENT INDIA

NUNDOLAL DEY

Published by

Gyan Publishing House
5, Ansari Road
Daryaganj, New Delhi-110002
Phone: 011-47034999, 9811692060
E-mail: books@gyanbooks.com

Distribution Network
gyanbooks.com
India, USA, Canada, UK, Australia, France

ISBN : 978-81-212-2494-9 (HB)

2nd Impression 2021

Printed at: Gyan Press, Delhi.

Civilization in Ancient India
Author: Nundolal Dey

PREFACE.

The present work was originally published by me under the pseudonym of *Una* in a series of articles in the *Bengal Magazine* of 1877 and 1878. The favourable notice that was taken of them at the time by the leading journals of India has encouraged me to collect and present them to the public in a handy form. The present work therefore is almost a reprint of the articles in the *Bengal Magazine*, only that the verbal mistakes and palpable errors have been rectified and omissions supplied where necessary: I have attempted briefly in this work to deal with some of the subjects in which the ancient Hindus attained a high degree of excellence and to trace some of the causes of their decline. If this little book can excite in the mind of my reader any interest for India, past or present, I shall consider it not written in vain.

CHINSURAH,
October 14, 1902.

NUNDOLAL DEY.

CONTENTS.

demarkation between the ancient Hindus and the aborigines of the country, as is evidenced by many hymns of the *Rig-Veda:* "The waves of the Saraswati flow for our protection, she is for us like a town of iron;"* and "Destroy, Saraswati, the revilers of the gods, the offspring of the universal deluder, Brisaya; giver of sustenance, thou hast acquired for men the lands (seized by the *Asuras)*, and hast showered water upon them." "May the fierce Saraswati, riding in a golden chariot, the destructress of enemies, be pleased by our earnest laudation."†

We are not certain whether this migration was caused by over populousness or internal strife. It has been conjectured by some antiquarians that the latter must have been the probable cause, as the Indo-Aryans show in their earliest works a deadly hatred towards the *Asuras*, believed to have been the Ahasereus of ancient Iran. But it is certain that this was the first colonization of the Aryan nation, the flow of subsequent migration was towards the west. Thus the Panjab was the first abode of the Hindus, and their occupation of other parts of

---

* Translation in St. Martin's Geographie, as quoted by Mrs. Manning, in her *Ancient and Mediæval India.*

† Wilson's trans., Vol. III.

CIVILIZATION IN ANCIENT INDIA.

CHAPTER I.

ARTS.

All authorities agree that India is one of the earliest civilized countries in the world. The never-failing resources bestowed upon her by bountiful Nature supplied the wants of the people, and led them early to the cultivation of arts. It has been established by the researches of philology, for history which is comparatively a modern idea, does not lead us to those times of old, that the ancient Hindus were not the aborigines of the country. A colony of the Aryans, be their country Ariana or some other place in Central Asia, came by the pass of the Hindu Kush, and first settled themselves in the land which is bounded on the west by the river Kubha (the Kabul river) and on the east by the river Sindhu (the Indus). In the *Vaidic* period, we find their country extended and bounded on the north by the Himálaya, on the west by the river Kubha, on the south by the Sea, and on the east by the river Saraswati. The last mentioned river was the line of the country was subsequently made with the inorease of population.

The Aryan migration to India must have taken place at a very remote period. The testimony of language* of the Indo-Aryans and the wide difference of their alphabetical characters from those of the cognate languages, speak in favour of this conclusion. It is now, however, impossible to ascertain the exact period when the Aryans migrated from their primitive home in Central Asia.

The fruitful soil of the country which required only a trifling amount of labour for ample production, and the abundant stream's, supplied them with all the necessaries of life, and thus they were at their ease to devote themselves to higher contemplations, in which their brethren of Central Asia, not so favoured by nature, were far behind them. As the grafts when they are joined with vigorous stocks, show an earlier power of productiveness than the seedlings of the parent trce, so a colony when settled in a favourable soil, displays an earlier power of invention than their brethren of the mother-

* Professor Lassen is of opinion that as the word for plough, in western languages, is not derived from Zend or Sanskrit, it may be inferred that these nations separated before ploughs were known.

country. The varied features of the country, where Nature displays herself in all her grandeur, beauty and sublimity: its stupendous mountains, its mighty rivers, its extensive forests, its fruitful soil, its tropical climate,—all combined to make them a race of philosophers and poets. It is not strange, therefore, that their mind, under these circumstances, should have a proclivity towards religion.

By the lapse of time, the society was formed into a civil society, ruled over by a king, as is frequently mentioned in the *Vedas*. The constant wars of the ancient Hindus with the aborigines made them adept in the martial arts. With the increase of population, and the consequent extension of professions, the people were divided into four classes, restricting them and their descendants to follow a particular trade or profession. This was the origination of the system of caste, which, however detrimental it has become to the social welfare of their descendants in modern times, was introduced among them at the time and under the circumstances with an eye to general utility.

Thus an indigenous civilization grew up, which has done an immense amount of good to all other countries of the world, however unwittingly it may have been given by the Hindus, and however involuntarily it may have been taken by other nations. For civilization, like electricity, is diffusive, provided it gets a medium. Our ancient civilization, on the other hand, might have been affected by those of Egypt or Phœnicia, when we carried on trade with the people of those countries. But the Hindus have indeed civilised the neighbouring barbarous nations.

The knowledge of the ancient history of a country gives an impetus to the intellectual movement and accelerates the progress of its nation. The past must teach the present, and the present should elucidate the past. India, though poor at present, has an heirloom in its ancient glory; her sons have the prestige only of a line of illustrious ancestors. Nothing has now been left to them except to chant the praise of the adventurous heroes of the past. Yet when the incubus of inactivity shall pass away, this spirit of admiration shall contribute much to the regeneration of India. This indeed is a noble pride, which dignifies them the more in their fallen state.

There is no systematic history of India before the Mahomedan conquest: the facts are meagre and scattered. The *Rájatarangini* is the annals only of a single province. The antiquarian must grope his way through the gloom of ancient India by long and laborious researches. The facts and information which he would glean, should not only serve to unravel the skein of the past history of India, but also to inspire the people with noble aspirations when they would think upon the condition of their once glorious country: the past should be ransacked not for mere curiosity but for the present.

From the very earliest times, India has been celebrated as an agricultural, manufacturing, and commercial country. She not only grew the materials, worked upon them, but sold them in different parts of the then known world. At one period she held the monopoly of trade both in the Indian Ocean and in the Eastern Seas. She had no rival to compete with her: Egypt had not then learned to trade. Even so early as the period of the *Rig-Veda*, the Hindus are mentioned to have been a sea-going people. They knew the art of ship-building. It was only after the time of Sankarácharjya in the eighth century of the Christian era when Bráhminism triumphed over Buddhism, that a ban was placed upon the ocean as on other things to check the freedom of idea inculcated by the latter religion.

Both native and foreign writers testify that the ancient Hindus were a commercial and sea-going people. Not only the *Rig-Veda*,* but also the Institutes of Manu,† and the writings of the Buddhistic period abundantly prove that they navigated the ocean for commercial purposes; Arrian, Strabo,‡ Pliny, Ptolemy, Fa Hian and other foreign writers, speak also to the same effect. They traded in Burma, Sumatra, China, and the Eastern Archipelago in the East; in the West their intercourse was principally with the Arabs, Egyptians, and the nations of Eastern Africa. They colonized Java§ and the neighbouring islands. Their principal ports were Barygaza, (where Arrian sojourned, while a

---

* "And Bhujyu, who sailed in a hundred-oared ship, and went to sea, and was nearly drowned, they (the Aswins) brought back in vessels of their own along the bed of the ocean." See Wilson's trans., Vol. I; And "Merchants desirous of gain crowded the ocean with their ships." Wilson's trans., Vol. I.

† Chap. VIII, *Sloka* 157.

সমুদ্রযানকুশলা দেশকালার্থ দর্শিনঃ।
স্থাপয়ন্তি তু যাং বৃদ্ধিং সা তত্রাধিগমং প্রতি ॥

And again in *Sloka* 406 of the same chapter:

দীর্ঘাধ্বনি যথাদেশং যথাকালং তরোভবেৎ।
নদী তীরেষু তদ্বিদ্যাৎ সমুদ্রে নাস্তি লক্ষণং ॥

‡ "The admiral lets out ships for hire to those who undertake voyages and traffic as merchants." Book XV. Ch. I.

§ Hamilton's *Gazetteer*, and *Journal of the Asiatic Society* 1873, "*On the History of Pegu.*"

commercial agent), Musiris, Kalliane, Mausalipatam, Támralipta and other towns. Spices, ivory, ebony, precious stones, pearls silken and cotton goods, were the articles, which they supplied to the civilized nations of Europe, Asia, and Africa. "Ivory, garments, armour, spices and peacocks"* found their way from India† to the court of Solomon. She fed the luxury of the Romans, and thus her trade may be said to have been one of the indirect causes which led to the downfall of the Empire. The great Buddhist monarch, Asoka, sent an ambassador to the king of Ceylon, who embarked in a vessel from the port of Támralipta.‡

The ancient Hindus must have carried on an overland trade with the nations of Western Asia and Europe. Manu speaks of their knowledge of foreign countries and of their land journeys. The Persians of the time of Herodotus bartered with the Hindu merchants who came to their country with hordes of camels laden with merchandise. Wilford speaks of Hindu temples at Mahá Jowállá Mukhee§ in the neighbourhood of

* "These birds were so rare in Greece that a male and female were valued at Athens at a thousand drachmæ or £32 5*s*. 10*d*. sterling."—*Indian Miscellany*.

† Max Muller's *Science of Language*.

‡ Klaproth's *Notes on Fa Hian's Travels*.

§ *Asiatic Researches*, Vol. V.

Baku on the western border of the Caspian Sea, where Praun Poory, a Fakir, went to pay his homage during the latter part of the eighteenth century; he saw many Hindus residing at Astrachan; on the coast of the Black Sea also a Hindu temple existed where pilgrims from India generally frequented. We cannot indeed account for the existence of the Hindus and Hindu temples in places so distant from India, unless we consider them to be the relics of the commercial enterprise of the ancient Hindus. There is mention of an ambassador being sent with presents to Augustus Cæsar by an Indian king, Pandion, or according to others, Porus. He was accompanied by a Gymno-sophist who, like Calanus, burnt himself to death at Athens. They took the overland route best known to the Hindu merchants, for Nicolaus Damascenus states that "at Antioch, near Daphne, he met with ambassadors from the Indians, who were sent to Augustus Cæsar."*

Thus India became immensely rich by her trade: she was considered the *El Dorado* of the East by foreign nations. It was indeed this idea which raised the cupidity of Semiramis, Cyrus,

* Strabo, Book XV, Ch. I. Hamilton & Falconer's trans.

Darius, Alexander, Genghis and Timur for the invasion of India. The Egyptians, Phœnicians, Greeks and Arabs were attracted by the report of her riches to crowd in her coasts for commercial purposes.

The ancient Hindus had learnt the arts of agriculture, weaving, and cart-making long before the period of the Rig-Veda. They had ploughs, for there are many passages which show that ploughing was used for the purpose of sowing rice, barley and other food-grains; the gods were invoked for the purpose of protecting the fields and making them pleasant;* and hymns were chanted to the sowing season:

"May the heavens, the waters, the firmament, be kind to us; may the lord of field be gracious to us; let us undeterred (by foes) have recourse to him.

"May the oxen (draw) happily, the men labour happily,......may the traces bind happily, wield the goad happily."†

The fields were measured with a rod, and they carried the products home in carts, which were generally made of Dalbergia Sisu. Carpenters‡ are frequently mentioned, who "bent

* Wilson's trans. Vol. I.
† Wilson's trans. Vol. III.
‡ Wilson's trans. Vol. I.

the pliant metal round the wheel," and constructed not only their carts but also their war chariots. From the interest and anxiousness displayed for fields and cattle it seems that during the Vaidic period agriculture was the general profession; only the surplus products after consumption were sold in different trading places. It was not till after the expiration of a long period, when population had largely increased and the profession had greatly extended, that Manu assigned the art of cultivation to a certain section of the community. The Hindus evidently made great progress in the art at the time of the author of the Institutes, for among the enumeration of the several kinds of production, we find the names of rice, pulses, sugar-cane, sesamum, barley, mustard, flax and cotton, some of which were not known to the Hindus of the preceding age. Eratosthenes, and Megasthenes who resided as an ambassador in the court of Chandragupta, state that the people were acquainted with the rotation of crops.*

Weaving is as old as agriculture: they both belong to pre-historic times. Weavers and spinners are mentioned in the Rig-Veda.† Manu

---

* Strabo, Book XV.

† Wilson's trans. Vol. II.

speaks of cotton, flax and woollen cloths, and cloths coloured with safflower and lac-dye.* Cotton was unknown to the Greeks of the fifth century before the Christian era, for Herodotus states with a sort of wonder that "They (the Hindus) possess likewise a kind of plant, which instead of fruit, produces wool of a finer and better quality than that of sheep; of this the natives make their clothes."† The Indian cotton cloths were in very great requisition at Rome, which "in fineness of texture has never yet been approached in any other country." The silken cloths ‡ were manufactured since the time of Manu, the Rámáyana and the Mahábhárata speak of them. There cannot be any doubt that the art of extracting silk from cocoons were, in ancient times, known only to the Scythians and the Hindus. The latter made such improvement in the art of making silken fabrics, that they challenged the admiration of the emperors of Rome, and Justinian sent for the "silkworms' eggs" to Serica-India (Serhind) for the purpose of introducing them into Europe.

In mineralogy, India gives the palm to no country on the surface of the earth. Gold, silver,

---

* Chap 10, Slokas 87 and 89.

† Beloc's Herodotus, Book III.

‡ Chap. 10, Sloka 87.

iron and copper abound in many provinces. The diamond, sapphire and other precious stones are found in various districts. It was known to the Hindus of the Vaidic period. Manu says that "the king should take half the portion for the protection of the mines, because he is the lord of the land."* The Hindus of the Rig-Veda period had a knowledge of metallurgy; for even in that earliest time we find them possessed of metallic weapons and ornaments :—

"Lances (gleam), Maruts, upon your shoulders, anklets on your feet, golden cuirasses on your breasts, pure (waters shine) in your chariots; lightnings, blazing with fire, glow in your hands, and golden tiaras are towering on your head."† We also find them "wearing beautiful rings," and carrying "axes" and "hatchets." Iron wheel-rims and "iron leg" are also mentioned. At the time of Manu, they made ornaments and plates of gold, silver and copper: there were instruments also for agricultural and domestic purposes. Subsequently at tho time of the Rámáyana and the Mahábhárata, we see that they had made very great improvements in working upon metal for various purposes.

* Chap. 7, Sloka 39.
† Wilson's Trans. Vol. III.

Foreign writers also attest to the existence of their rich mines; Herodotus speaks of their mines of gold and of the wonderful ants which were the guardians, as it were, of these mines. Later Greek writers considered that some of the streams of the country literally rolled down dust of gold, especially the Eranaboas (the River Sone).* Nearchus speaks of their use of brass which was cast and not wrought. The great Iron pillar at Delhi, which by some is considered to have been transfixed to the earth by king Dhava, and according to others by Prithiraj, for judging the destiny of India, excites our wonder when we think of their enormous "furnaces, foundries and forges," and the magnitude of the levers which must have been used for raising it before transfixion. The filagree works of Cuttack and Dacca, which have been known to the Hindus for hundreds of years, are admired by all nations of the world. In short, the knowledge of the ancient Hindus in mineralogy and metallurgy cannot be sufficiently admired. Their skill and their ingenuity in making metallic wares carry with them their own praise.

While we find that metallic ores abounded in

---

* Strabo says that in the territory of Sopeithes (the *Sawbiras*) "valuable mines both of gold and silver are situated."

the country, we cannot help considering whether coins were known to the ancient Hindus, for they display the advancement of a nation in civilization. We see indeed that metallic money is mentioned in their earliest works. The Rig-Veda speaks of golden *nishkas* :

"I, Kakshivat, unhesitatingly accepted a hundred nishkas."*

Manu speaks also of *nishkas, másakas* and *panas*. But still we find the ancient Hindus, like the Greeks of the Homeric period, using, in many instances, for exchange, their cattle (*Pasu, Pecus* whence the word *pecuniary*). Professor Goldstüker considers the *nishkas* to have been gold coins worn as necklaces; even in our time, we find such a custom in vogue especially among the people of the North-Western Provinces. The Rig-Veda speaks also of a coin called the *Hiranyapinda* (lump of gold). All this shows that coins were not in actual existence in the sense in which we use the term at present: stamped coins bearing the symbol of the king were not issued from the mint: but it seems that simple bullion was used for the sake of convenience. We are, however, borne out in our

---

* Wilson's trans. Vol. II.

statement by the standard which is given by Manu for estimating the value of a coin :—

8 *Trasarenus* (or motes)	= 1 *Licksha* (or poppy seed).
3 *Liksahs*	= 1 *Rajasarshapa* (or Black mustard seed).
4 *Rajasarshapas*	= 1 *Goursarshapa* (or White mustard seed).
6 *Goursarshapas*	= 1 *Java* (or Barleycorn).
3 *Javas*	= 1 *Krishnal* (or *Rattika*).
5 *Krishnals*	= 1 *Masha*.
16 *Mashas*	= 1 *Suvarna*.
4 *Suvarnas*	= 1 *Nishka*.*

and

Silver weighing

2 *Krishnals*	= 1 Silver *Másaka*.
16 *Másakas*	= 1 *Dharana* or silver *Purana*.†

And again

Copper weighing

1 *Suvarna*	= 1 *Pana*

It is very clear therefore that the value of ancient money depended upon the weight it bore. It seems, however, that coined money was not issued till the time of Ráma, king of Ajodhyá,

* Chap. VIII. Slokas 133, 134 and 137.
† Ibid, Slokas 135 and 136.

when the people had made very great advancement in the art of engraving. *Nishkas* are often mentioned in the Rámáyana, and there still exists a popular tradition that Ráma had coined money, and those that can be had are retained with avidity and worshipped. But this is our conjecture, the history of ancient Hindu coinage is much immersed in obscurity; the earliest Hindu coins which have been discovered by the researches of numismatists do not date back beyond the fifth century before the Christian era.

Besides the manufactures which we have mentioned before, the Hindus were acquainted with the manufacturing of salt and sugar from a very remote antiquity. According to Hamilton, sugar was introduced from India into Arabia, and from thence into Europe and Africa. In fact the derivation of *sugar* favors the supposition that this commodity was introduced from India into the western countries.* Nearchus testifies to their knowledge of making paper. The Hindus were early acquainted with the art of brewing, and at the time of Manu they could distil various sorts of wine. We do not cer-

* "The Sanskrit word for Sugar is *Sarkara*, whence the Persian *Shakar* and *Shakkar*, tho Arabic *Sokkar*, the Greek *Sakkhar*, the Latin *Saccharum*."

tainly like to contest the invention of glass with any other country, but certain it is that the Hindus of the time of the Mahábhárata were acquainted with the art of glass making: the crystal floor in the palace of Indraprastha deluded Duryodhana, and there are other books where crystal gates, and mirrors are mentioned.*

We have thus enumerated only the important of the several manufacturing and industrial arts with which India was early acquainted. We shall now proceed to consider the other phases in her ancient civilization.

The scene of the Rig-Veda opens to our view not a race of savages living in caves with bears or pachyderms, or flaying the mammoth with their chert flints for the purpose of feasting upon its raw flesh, or roving in the wilderness in a state of nature, but a nation already advanced in civilization and acquainted with the necessary arts of life. They lived not upon stalls erected in the midst of waters like the Indians

---

* Bhágabata, Skandha 8, Chap. XV, Sloka 16. European writers generally ascribe the authorship of the work to Bopa Deva, the grammarian, who flourished in the twelfth century of the Christian era, but the supposition has been ably refuted by Baboo Ram Das Sen in an article on "Bopa Deva" in the *Bándhaba*. And see also Vishnu Purána, Part II. Chapter II. Sloka 19, and Máhábhárata, Bhishma Parva, Chap. V.

of America, but they dwelt in houses of masonry-works, though not in palaces. They had their knives, swords and lances; they had their clothes made of cotton to cover them; they had the productions of the soil to live upon; they had their carts and waggons for conveyance; they had their towns to dwell in, and roads to saunter about. But there existed no temples at the time, but each dwelling was furnished with a room as a receptacle of the sacred fire.

By the lapse of time an improved system in the art of architecture was introduced. Manu mentions six kinds of forts,* and he advises the king to prefer the hill-fort, which must be large enough to hold arms, ammunitions and machines, and should be protected with high walls, and should contain garden and rooms allotted to various purposes.† Beside the forts, there were houses and temples, gardens, and orchards, tanks and wells lined with steps. Later at the time of Válmiki, we can have some idea of the towns by his description of Ayodhyá in the Rámáyana, which could vie with any city of modern times in splendour and beauty:—

---

* Chap. VII, Sloka 70.

† Chap. VII, Slokas 75 and 76.

There (in the kingdom of Kosala) the celebrated town of Ayodhyá is situated, built by Manu himself, the king of men. It is twelve *yoyans* in length and three in breadth. The streets and high roads are regular, and they are adorned with well-blown flowers and frequently watered. It is ornamented with gates and porticoes and lined with shops. It contains all sort of arms and machines. It is dwelt by artizans and the professional chanters of praise. It is beautiful and brilliant. It contains lofty houses adorned with banners, and it is protected with *Sataghnis.* Everywhere in the town there are houses for the ballet-girls; there are gardens and mangoe-topes. The forts are surrounded by deep and impassable moats, and they are inaccessible to enemies. It is crowded with elephants, horses, kine, camels, and mules. In some parts the feudatory chiefs crowd with their presents; merchants from various countries live in it. In some parts the walls studded with gems are resplendent as the mountains. There the houses for amusement exist; and in some parts dwell the public women. In some places the town is adorned with seven-storied houses embellished with all sorts of gems. There the houses are close and placed on the same level. It is stored with rice and other grains, and the water is like the juice of the sugar-cane. The whole town resounds to the music of the tabor, flute and harp. It is the abode of all good men as the heavens of the beatified persons; and it is dwelt by myriads of intrepid warriors, who do not raise their hands against the helpless and the unprotected, but who kill by the might of their arms and with sharp instruments the fierce, growling lions, tigers and boars of the forests.*

Mosaic work was therefore evidently known to the Hindus as early as the period of the Rámáyana. Balconies and oriels are mentioned in the Mahábhárata.

Modern India does not possess any architectural remains of the classic period; the structures that exist at present do not date back beyond the third century before the Christian era. The pillars which were erected by Asoka in different parts of the country for the promulgation of the edicts of Buddhism, are the earliest that have yet been observed. The *Mrichchhakatika Nátaka* of king Sudraka, who flourished in the first century, gives us an accurate deli-

* Rámáyana, Bálakánda, Chap. V.

neation of the houses during the Buddhistic period: Basantasena's house is most minutely described, which shows an evident advancement in taste and knowledge of the mediæval Hindus in the art of architecture. The rock-cut structures of Southern India are so amazing that "the first European observers could not find terms sufficiently intense to express their wonder and admiration." These edifices were scooped out of solid rocks and formed into fanes, images, colonnades, and courts. The cave-temples of Ajanta, Karli, Ellora and Elephanta were formed in this manner. Though the Hindus never attained a high degree of perfection in sculpture like the ancient Greeks, yet some of their sculptural works especially in the temple of Ajanta are admired by all observers. The exquisite carvings, and the beautiful arabesques, frets, and scrolls which are found in these temples, evince their attainment of high skill in this branch of architecture. The columns are of different sorts, and the mouldings are beautiful, rich and varied. There are other styles of architecture found in Orissa, Behar and Rajputana. The structures are lofty, and of "unrivalled taste and beauty." Minute accounts of ancient Hindu architecture are given in Fergusson's *History of Architecture*, Ram Raz's *Essay on Hindu Architecture*, and the *Mánsára*, the most important of Hindu *Silpa-sástras* extant in the South.

Architecture is a sure test of a nation's civilization. We wonder not so much at the skill, taste, genius and imagination of the ancient Hindus, as at their patience and assiduity which they have displayed in cutting away chip after chip of stone with their chisel to bring out temples, effigies, pillars and arches. Our civilization doubtless possesses a knowledge of many things unknown and undreamt of by the people of far-back ages, but, on the other hand, how many things may have belonged to their civilization which are lost to us! The so-called "barbarism" of the ancients has left behind it a permanent monumental defiance (as for instance the pyramids of Egypt) to all the arts and skill of this age of civilization. We are indeed lost in wonder when we think of the patience of the ancient Hindus, which could make up for their ignorance of the inventions of modern science.

Thus we see that during the Vaidic period there were agriculturists, weavers, black-smiths, carpenters, goldsmiths and forgers; as well as perfumers, painters, confectioners, actors, jewellers, ivory-workers, and stone-cutters.* At the time of Manu, there existed besides those whom we have already mentioned, joiners, architects, miners, dyers, musicians, tanners and lapidaries. There existed also courts of Justice, way-side inns, gardens, wine-shops, taverns, assembly-rooms, artizan's shops and pastry-shops. At the time of the Rámáyana, the Hindus had learnt mosaic work and engraving.† They also knew to make slippers and umbrellas. During the period of the Mahábhárata, they were acquainted with the art of glass-making: they also made very great improvement in architecture, dyeing and weaving. Subsequently we find them to be sculptors and carvers.

The Hindus had always been renowned as a nation of warriors. It is only since the conquest of the whole of India by the Mahomedans that they have lost that time-honored celebrity. Accustomed from the very earliest times to wars and conquests, they had received a thorough knowledge of military arts and tactics.

---

* These names are mentioned in the Yayur Veda: see Proceedings of the Asiatic Society of Bengal, April, 1869.

† দদৌ তস্য ততঃ প্রীতিঃ স্বনামাঙ্কোপশোভিতম্।
অঙ্গুরীয়মভিজ্ঞানং রাজপুত্র্যাঃ পরন্তপঃ॥
Rámáyana, Kánda 4, Chap. 44.

Since their migration into India, they had constant engagements with the aborigines for occupation of land. Necessity made them learn many things of the military art, which they otherwise would not have learnt. Even so early as the time of the Rig-Veda, we find their armies divided into infantry and charioteers. The men were all accoutred in coats of mail, and they fought with bows, arrows, lances, axes and quoits.

The Hindus were always celebrated as connoisseurs of horse-flesh, their "raging and champing" steeds were richly caparisoned, and they bestowed all precious care upon them when they did not use them in battle.

Stimulating themselves with the juice of the *Soma*, and invoking the gods they entered into the field of battle. The use of elephants was not known during the Vaidic period.

A detailed account of the ancient military arrangements of the Hindus is given in the seventh chapter of Manu. The whole army was divided into four classes: the infantry, the cavalry, the chariots, and the elephants. The drilling and the superintendence of the army were placed in the hands of the general,* who

* Sl. 65.

was bound to practise the soldiers and the animals every day.* The king is advised, when desiring to attack his enemy's country, to set out in his campaign in winter or spring. Eight sorts of manœuvers are mentioned in case of attack by the enemy.† Various kinds of arrangements the king is advised to make of his troops while engaged in battle, and follow the plan laid down for conducting a siege of the enemy's fortress.‡ It seems that the inhabitants of Kurukshetra, Matsya, Surasena, and Panchála were famed at the time of the Code for their stalwart frame and courage, for the soldiers from those countries were required to be placed foremost in the rank of battle.

The principles of war which are laid down in the *Institutes* were dictated by a spirit of humanity and manliness. Whatever may be said of the military tactics of the ancient Hindus, cowardice formed no part of their element. No breath of calumny can attaint our forefathers for want of true manliness and magnanimity of the heart. To accept the gauntlet was the motto of an ancient Hindu warrior however strong the adversary might

* Sl. 102.

† Sls 187, 188, 19'

‡ Sls. 195, 196.

be,* not to retreat from battle was conducive of prosperity. The kings, who fight with their utmost strength actuated by a desire of killing each other, without the idea of retreating, surely go to heaven.† Whoever being afraid flees from battle and is killed by the enemy obtains the sins of his master, and the little virtues which he has amassed, become the gain of his master.‡ That this was the idea of the later Hindus also, there cannot be any doubt, for cowardice in a Kshatriya is denounced in the *Mahábhárata* as one of the most culpable of offences, and to die in battle is pronounced to be the greatest of all virtues.

Warriors are prohibited to fight with barbed or poisoned arrows or arrows blazing with fire.§ Riders and charioteers should not fight with those who are on foot, or kill those who have asked for quarter. Warriors are also prohibited to attack those who are asleep, or unarmed, or

* Sl. 87.

† Sl. 89.

‡ Sls. 94 and 95 (chap. VII).

যস্তুভিতঃ পরাবৃত্তঃ সংগ্রামে হন্যতে পরৈঃ।
ভর্ত্তুর্যদ্দুষ্কৃতং কিঞ্চিৎ তৎ সর্ব্বং প্রতিপদ্যতে॥
যচ্চাস্য সুকৃতং কিঞ্চিদমুত্রার্থমুপার্জ্জিতং।
ভর্ত্তা তৎ সর্ব্বমাদত্তে পরাবৃত্তহতস্য তু॥

§ Sl. 90.

without armour, or spectators, or those who are broken down with grief, or who are wounded, or who are fleeing.*

Things plundered in battle belonged to those who got them.

With respect to the settlement of a country after it has been conquered, the king is advised to proclaim assurance of security to all its people: he is to elect a person from the old royal family as its king and frame laws for its government, but he should respect the customs of the country, and give him and his advisers valuable presents as token of respect,† that is, not make them feel their state of dependence.

Fighting on boats in rivers is mentioned both in the *Institutes* and the *Rámáyana*. From the time of Válmiki, wrestling and athletic exercises were as much prized as skill in shooting arrows.

The arms of the ancient Hindus were steel instruments of various size, shape and figure; but their principal implements of war were bows and arrows. In close battle, they generally fought with clubs, swords, and spears. They had other weapons which are metaphorically described, as the *Nágapása*, it seems, was nothing more than the lasso. The figure of their shields

* Sls. 92 and 93.

† Sls. from 201 to 204.

was long, narrow and convex, as may be observed in the frescoes at the Ajanta caves. The various descriptions we have in the *Rámáyana* and the *Mahábhárata* of arrows being vivified by the powers of charms, are accounted for even by the learned Hindus of our times, who are too learned to confound reality with poetic imagination, by considering that the arrow-heads were coated with chemical properties which would produce fumes or flames, like lucifer, by friction to the frame of the bow. We are not quite sure whether the Hindus at one time were so much advanced in the science of chemistry, but there can be no doubt that they possessed firearms. Their principal ordnance was the *Sataghni*, which was generally used for the protection of towns. Its very name indicates that it was the "killer of hundred." A description of it is given in the *Mahábhárata.**

পবিগৃহ্য শতঘ্নীশ্চ সচক্রাঃ সগুড়োপলাঃ ।
চিক্ষিপুঃ ভুজবেগেন লঙ্কামধ্যে মহাস্বনাঃ ॥

"They (the monkeys) taking the *Sataghnis* existent with wheels and balls of stone, and which produced tremendous noise, threw them into the midst of Lanka by the force of their

* *Vana Parva*, chap. 282.

arms." We have already seen that it is mentioned in the *Rámáyana.* The description gives the veritable picture of a modern cannon. In fact, Sir Arthur Cautley while excavating the Ganges canal came upon the site of an ancient town, seventeen feet below the ground, supposed to be the ancient town of Hastinápura, and found among other things a piece of ordnance closely resembling a small cannon.

Gunpowder therefore was evidently known to the ancient Hindus. It was known by the name of *Aurbágni,* being the invention of the Rishi Aurba.* The French can claim it as their own invention, the Chinese can also claim to be its independent inventors, but it is not at all surprising that another military nation as the ancient Hindus were, should have found out the nature and effect of the three most common substances of their own country. The ingredients and power of the "fire of Aurba" are thus described in the *Nítichintámani:*—

দশৈধং শোরকৈশ্চৈব পার্ব্বত্যাবীর্য্যমেব চ।
একীকৃত্যাংশভাগেন ক্রমাঙ্কু।সাষ্টবেদিতি ॥
দারুণো হুতভুক্তেন দহ্যতে সলিলাদিকং।†

* Aurba was the preceptor of Sagara, ancestor of Ráma.

† *Nítichintámani*, as quoted by Nundo Kumar Kabiratna in the *Nityadharmánuranjiká.*

"Combining burnt wood (charcoal), saltpetre, and sulphur by parts gradually lessened, a terrible fire is produced by which (even) water and others are burnt." There is a curious passage in the *Harivansa* in which both the gunpowder and the *Sataghni* are mentioned. Krishna while marching against Sálwa, put Dwa'rika, his capital, in a state of defence by

ঔর্ব্বাগ্নিং প্রোথিতং কৃত্বা শতঘ্নীং গুড়কৈর্যুতাং

"placing gunpowder under the ground, and loading the killer of hundred with balls."

During the many centuries which elapsed between the first colonization of the Hindus and their conquest by the Mahomedans in the twelveth century, India had never been subjugated though often she was invaded by foreign rulers. She was governed by her own kings and enjoyed her own laws. She elbowed out all her enemies. Semiramis escaped with twenty men only, and Cyrus with seven. The conquest of Darius Hystaspis does not appear to have extended beyond the Panjab. The strength and energy of Alexander's soldiers expended themselves in their battle with Porus. The king himself barely escaped with his life while attacking the Mallis. "The combat with Porus," says Plutarch, "abated the spirit of the Macedonians, and made them resolve to proceed no further in India. It was with difficulty they had defeated an enemy, who brought only twenty thousand foot and two thousand horse into the field; and therefore they opposed Alexander with great firmness when he insisted that they should pass the Ganges, which, they were informed, was thirty-two furlongs in breadth, and in depth a hundred fathom. The opposite shore too was covered with numbers of squadrons, battalions, and elephants. For the kings of the Gandarites and Prœsians were said to be waiting for them there, with eighty thousand horse, two hundred thousand foot, eight thousand chariots, and six thousand elephants trained to war."* The conquests of Seleucus and of Menander, the Bactrian king, of the north-western frontier, made but a temporary impression. The Hindus served in the army of Xerxes at the battle of Platea where they were disposed in opposition to the Hermionians, Eretrians, Styrians and Chalcidians; "their bows were made of reeds, as were also the arrows, which were pointed with iron, their leader was Pharnazathres, son of Artabates."†

* See Langhorne's Plutarch's *Lives: Alexander.*

† Herodotus, Books VII and IX.

The history of the Rajputs, especially those of Mewar, is a sequel to the glorious history of ancient India. Their heroism was like the flash of the flickering lamp before extinction. From the time of Bappa who conquered Chitore in 728 A.D. to that of Udaya Sing who was expelled from it in 1568, they displayed such courage and heroism as were only worthy of the descendants of Ráma. The Spartan matrons would have quailed beneath the stern look of the Rajput mothers. When dressed in yellow the Rajput warriors never turned their backs against the enemy: it was a sin of the blackest dye. Their undaunted courage was shared by the females of their household. The *Johur* (self-burning) of Padmini, Karnávati, and myriads of Rajput ladies; the heroic deeds of Jawáhir Bái, and the mother of Puttun and of her daughter-in-law will be remembered with wonder and admiration.* Though the Rajputs were indeed defeated and killed by their Mahomedan conquerors, yet it was a defeat which equals any great victory recorded in the history of the world! They knew it was better to die than to live in ignominy and subjection. The tradition

---

* Tod's *Rájasthán : History of Mewár.*

of their heroic exploits feeds the memory of their descendants: though distanced by centuries they move among us in spirit; though cut off by death, they live in glory!

Even the Bengalis were once a martial nation. It is as true as their present degenerated condition. Amidst the gloom that pervades the history of Bengal before the Mahomedan conquest, we have the glimmerings of inscriptions and occasional records of Buddhistic writers to attest to their former greatness. They had attained their highest state of prosperity during the administration of the Pál dynasty. They, under Deva Pála Deva, had "conquered the earth from the source of the Ganges as far as the well known bridge which was constructed by the enemy of *Dasàsya*, from the river of Lokeecool (present Lukhipore) as far as the Ocean of the habitation of Varuna."* And again the Buddal inscription makes mention of their conquests: "Trusting to whose (the minister Kedára Misra's) wisdom the lord of Gauda for a long time enjoyed the surface of the sea-girt earth by eradicating the race of the Utkalas, conquering the haughtiness of the Hunas, and humbling the

---

* Inscription on a copperplate found at Monghyr: translated by Charles Wilkins, *Asiatic Researches*, Vol. I.

pride of the kings of Gurjjara and Dravida."* Even if we consider these to be exaggerations, the inscribers must have had good grounds for their statements. Judging from their present condition, it may sound strange that they could have marched armies beyond the Indus or the Vindhya range, but these inscriptions are no modern forgeries, and their antiquity has been established beyond the shadow of a doubt.

---

* It is the translation of the following stanza of the Buddal Pillar inscription by Babu Pratápachandra Ghosha, B.A. See Journal of the Asiatic Society of Bengal, 1874 :—

উত্‌কীলিতোত্‌কলকুলং হৃতহূনগর্ব্বং
খর্ব্বীকৃতদ্রবিড়গুর্জ্জররাজদর্পং।
ভূপীঠমব্ধিরসনাভরণং বুভোজ—
গৌড়েশ্বরশ্চিরমুপাস্য ধিয়াং যদীয়াং॥

CHAPTER II.

SCIENCES.

The originality of some of the Hindu sciences has been acknowledged by all eminent scientists who have devoted their attention to an inquiry into the intellectual advancement of the people of ancient India. Progress is not only the law of man, but the peculiar characteristic of science. But however indistinct the Hindus might have been at first with respect to some of their conclusions, or however palpable might have been the foreign elements in some of their later works, their progress was marvellous, and it must be admitted that the world owes much to ancient India for its present advancement in the knowledge of science.

The science of Astronomy, which ennobles the heart and the intellect, was the branch to which they especially devoted their thoughts even at the earliest times. To every Veda is appended a "sort of astronomical treatise, the object of which is to explain the adjustment of the calendar, for the purpose of fixing the proper periods for the performance of religious duties." Even Mr. Bentley, the most inveterate opponent of the Hindus in their "pretentions" to antiquity, acknowledges that their division of the ecliptic into twenty-seven lunar mansions was made 1442 years before the Christian era.* The earliest writer on astronomy is said to have been Parásara. "Although it is generally supposed that the *Súrya-siddhánta* is the oldest (of the eighteen astronomical works), yet some consider the *Brahma-siddhánta* to be so; and it is stated in the *Sambhu-horáprakása* (an astrological work), that the *Soma-siddhánta* is the first, the *Brahma-siddhánta* the second, and the *Súrya-siddhánta* the third in the order of time. But this opinion is not generally received."† Besides these books, Varáha surnamed *Mihira* or the Sun from his knowledge of astronomy, wrote the *Varáhi-sanhitá* at the latter end of the fifth century;‡ Árya Bhatta, author of the *Áryabháṭiya-Sutra*, flourished during the same period; and the *Siddhánta-siromani* was written by Bháskarácharjya, who, according to his own statement, was born in the year 1036 of the

* Elphinstone's *History of India*, Book III, Ch. I.

† Pandit Bápu Deva Sástri's Postscript to his Translation of the *Surya-siddhánta*.

‡ *Asiatic Researches*, Vol. II, p. 391.

Sálivάhana era, *i. e.*, A.D. 1114, and composed the work when he was thirty-six years old.*

The principal objects of Hindu astronomy were the rectification of the calendar, the ascertainment of the chronological epochs, and the calculation of the eclipses.

According to the notions of the ancient Hindus the form of the Earth is perfectly round: it has no supporter, but stands firmly in the expanse of heaven by its own inherent force.† Instead of the earth moving round the sun, the sun moves round it. "The property of attraction is inherent in the earth. By this property the earth attracts any unsupported heavy things towards it. The thing appears to be falling [but it is in a state of being drawn to the earth]. The ethereal expanse being equally outspread all around, where can the earth fall?"‡ Thus we see that the attraction of gravitation was known to Bháskarácharjya! The sun by his diurnal motion causes day and night, he does neither rise nor set, but when he is first seen, he is said to rise, and when he

---

* *Siddhánta-siromani*, Chap. XIII, Sl. 58.

† *Siddhánta-siromani*, Chap. III, Sl. 2.—Wilkinson's Translation; *Goladhyaya*.

‡ Ibid. Sl. 6.

disappears, he is said to set.* When it is noon at one place, it is midnight at the place where a line, drawn straight from the sun through *Sumeru* to the opposite side, terminates. This *Sumeru* is nothing more than the axis of the earth, for "the golden mountain Meru," says the author of the *Súrya-siddhánta* "containing heaps of various precious stones, passes through the middle of the terrestrial globe (as an axis projecting on both sides at the poles)."†

The sun in his annual motion through the signs of the zodiac causes the variations in the seasons,‡ which are six in number. The zodiacal circle is divided into twelve parts, and therefore it is called *Ráshi-vritta*; it is also divided into twenty-seven parts, and therefore it is called *nakshatra-vritta*. Each *Ráshi* or sign is again divided into thirty degrees *(ansas)*; therefore the whole circle consists of three hundred and sixty degrees. The twelve lunar months correspond to the twelve signs of the zodiac, and they are named according to the situation of the sun.§ The lunar mansions are mentioned in the earliest hymns of the Veda, being of Indian

* *Vishnu Purána*, Part II, Ch. 8, Sl. 15.

† Trans. by Pandit Bápu Deva Sástri, Chap. 12, Sl. 34.

‡ *Vishnu Purána*, Part II, Ch. 10, Sl. 21, and Ch. 11, Sl. 6.

§ *Surya-siddhánta*, Ch. I, Sl. 48—note by the translator.

origin, whereas the solar signs of the zodiac were, according to Dr. Bhau Dáji and Mr. Colebrooke, borrowed by the Hindus from the Greeks. When the sun enters the sign of Makara (Capricorn), it becomes *Uttaráyana* or the winter solstice, and *Dakshináyana* or summer solstice when he enters the sign of Karkata (Cancer). The equinoxes are called *Vishuvas*. The days and nights become equal when he enters the equinoxes. After the sun has passed the vernal equinox, the day becomes longer than the night, and after the autumnal equinox, it becomes shorter.

The Hindu astronomers mapped out the starry heaven into different constellations.* Among them, may be mentioned, the *Sisumára* or the Ursa minor, and the *Saptarshimandala* or the Ursa major. At the tail of the former the *Dhruvanakshatra* or the Pole-star is situated. The sun, moon, and other planets, and the stars are revolving round the Dhruva, being bound to it by the cord of the atmosphere,† and the star itself is said to be rotating in its place along with the planetary system.‡ The *Súrya-*

* The Rig-Veda speaks of Orion (*Prajápati*) and Aldebaran (*Rohini*).

† *Vishnu Purána*, Part II, Ch. 12, Sls. 26, 27.

‡ Ibid. Ch. 9, Sls. 1-3.

siddhánta gives the cause of the planetary motions: "The Deities, invisible (to human sight) named Síghrochcha (*i. e.* the farthest point from the centre of the earth in the orbit of each of the planets), Mandochcha (Apogees) and Páta (Nodes) consisting of (continuous and endless) time, being situated at the ecliptic, produce the motions of the planets. The Deities, (Sighrochcha and Mandochcha) attract the planets (from their uniform course) fastened by the reins of winds borne by the Deities towards themselves to the east or west, with their right or left hands according as they are to their right or left. (Besides this) a (great) wind called *Pravaha* carries the planets (westward) which are also attracted towards their apogees. Thus the planets being attracted (at once) to the east and west get the various motions."*

They had a correct view of the cause of tides. That they are caused by the influence of the moon they had no doubt, "as the water in a plate becomes inflated by the heat of the fire, so the water of the ocean increases by the waxing of the moon. At other times, there is no increase or decrease of the water of the ocean,

* *Súrya-siddhánta*, Ch. II, Sls. 1, 2, 3—Sástri's Trans

except in the white or black fortnight of the moon at the time of her rising or setting, when the decrease or increase is observed. The water of the ocean is seen to increase or decrease five hundred and ten fingers (*i. e.* twenty-one and one-fourth cubits) (by the influence of the moon)."* The moon like the other planets moves round the earth. She has got no light of her own, but reflects only the borrowed rays of the sun. "This ball of nectar the moon being in contact with rays of the sun, is always illuminated by her shinings on that side turned towards the sun. The side opposite to the sun, dark as the raven black locks of a young damsel, is obscured by being in its own shadow, just as that half of a water-pot which is turned from the sun, is obscured by its own shadow. At the conjunction, the moon is between us and the sun: and its lower half, which is then visible

---

* *Vishnu Purána*, Part II, Ch. 4, Sls. 90–92.

স্থালিস্থমগ্নি সংযোগাদুদ্রেকি সলিলং যথা।
তথেন্দুবৃদ্ধৌ সলিলমম্ভোধৌ মুনিসত্তম!॥
ন ন্যূনা নাতিরিক্তাশ্চ বর্দ্ধন্ত্যাপো হ্রসন্তি চ।
উদয়াস্তমনেম্বিন্দোঃ পক্ষয়ো শুক্লকৃষ্ণয়োঃ॥
দশোত্তরাণি পঞ্চৈব অঙ্গুলানাং শতানি বৈ।
অপাং বৃদ্ধিক্ষয়ৌ দৃষ্টৌ সামুদ্রীণাং মহামুনে!॥

and see also *Raghuvansa*, Ch. V, Sl. 61.

to the inhabitants of the earth, being turned from the sun is obscured in darkness. The half again of the moon when it has moved to the distance of six signs from the sun, appears to us at the period of full moon brilliant with light."†

By whatever metaphorical way the Pauranics might have attempted to explain most of the phenomena of heaven, and consequently plunged them into the deepest obscurity, it is satisfactory to observe that the authors from whom they derived their knowledge of the science, afford us a reasonable and perspicuous explanation of them. Thus in elucidating the theory of the eclipses, the Pauranics have brought forth demons to suit the simple minds of the mass of the people, and therefore instead of enlightening the world, as they professedly intend to do, they have thrown it into a state of confusion and superstition. But the *Surya-siddhánta* sees Ráhu and Ketu in no other light than simply as the ascending and descending nodes. According to it, the solar eclipse is the interception of the light of the sun by the moon's intervention between him and the earth; and the lunar eclipse takes place when the moon moving eastward enters

---

† *Goládhyáya* of the *Siddhánta-siromani*: Wilkinson's Trans. Ch. X, Sls. 1, 2.

the earth's shadow, which is of a conical form, and extends to a distance considerably beyond that of the moon's orbit. Both the *Súrya-siddhánta* and the *Siddhánta-siromani** give full particulars for calculating everything connected with the eclipses.

The Hindu astronomers had no idea of the universal law of gravitation, but Bháskaráchárjya, as we have mentioned before, was acquainted with the attractive force of the earth: he not only says that all heavy unsuspended bodies are drawn to the earth by the force inherent to it, but states also "that those who are placed at the distance of half the earth's circumference from each other, are mutually antipodes, as a man on the bank of a river and his shadow reflected in the water: but as well those who are situated at the distance of 90° as those who are situated at that of 180° from you, maintain their position without difficulty. They stand with the same ease as we do here in our position."†

Besides the Sun, Moon, and the Earth, other planets were known to the ancient Hindus: Mars, Mercury, Jupiter, Venus and Saturn were known

* *Súrya-siddhánta*, Ch. IV, and *Goládhyáya* of the *Siddhánta-siromani*, Ch. VIII.

† Wilkinson's Translation of the *Goládhyáya* of the *Siddhánta-siromani*, Ch. III, Sl. 10.

respectively by the name of Mangala, Budha, Vrihaspati, Sukra, and Sani. They revolve round the earth; and move in their orbits towards the west with the same velocity. The places of the stars and planets were ascertained by a reference to the meridian of Lanká, which passed through Rohitaka, Ujjaini, Kurukshetra and the North Pole.

The instruments* which were used by the astronomers, are *Bhubhagola* or the Armillary sphere, *Kapálayantra* or the Clepsydra, and the Sand-clock: these instruments were used for measuring time;† *Sanku* (called also *Narayantra*) or the gnomon; *Yashti* or the staff, *Dhanu* or semicircle, *Chakra* or circle; these are dial instruments. Besides these, Bháskaráchárjya mentions the following: *Nádi-Valaya* or the equinoctial, *Turiya* or quadrant; *Phalaka-yantra* invented by Bháskaráchárjya himself; *Dhi-yantra* or the genius-instrument, *Swayanavaha-yantra*

---

* *Súrya-siddhánta*, Ch. XIII.

† The measure of time is thus given in the *Súrya-siddhánta*:—

6 Pránas (a Prána being 4 seconds)	= 1 Pala.
60 Palas	= 1 Ghatiká.
60 Ghatikás	= 1 Nakshatra Ahorátra (sidereal day and night).
30 (Nakshatra) Ahorátras	= 1 Nakshatra Mása.
30 Sávana (terrestrial) days	= 1 Sávana month,

a terrestrial day being reckoned from sunrise to sunrise.

or self-revolving instrument, and the syphon. The descriptions of these instruments and the purposes for which they were used, are fully given in the *Siddhánta-siromani.** But strange to say we do not find among these instruments anything like a telescope.

Previous to the time of Sawai Jayasinha, king of Amber,—who devoted his life to the study of the sciences, reformed the calendar, and constructed a new set of tables, which, in honour of the reigning sovereign, was entitled *Zeej Mahomedshahy,*—it seems that an observatory existed at Oujein He found that the calculations of the places of stars, as obtained from the tables in common use, were widely different from those determined by observation. He therefore constructed five observatories at Delhi, Muttra, Oujein, Benares and Jeypore, containing instruments of masonry works of his own invention, "as the brass instruments did not come up to the ideas he had formed of their accuracy, because of the smallness of their size, the want of division into minutes, the shaking and wearing of their axes, the displacement of the centres of the circles, and the shifting of the planes of the

---

* Ch. XI, Wilkinson's Trans.

instrument."* He therefore caused the following instruments to be made: *Jeypergas, Ram Yantra,* and *Samrát Yantra* (or the prince of instruments) by which the meridional distance and the declination and the right ascension of a heavenly body, may be known. In the Benares observatory, the instruments, a detailed description of which is given by the Rev. M. A. Sherring,† are the *Bhittiyantra* or Mural Quadrant for ascertaining the sun's altitude and zenith distance at noon, and his greatest declination, and the latitude of the place; the *Samrát Yantra,* the *Digansayantra* for finding the degrees of azimuth of a planet or star, and other instruments mentioned by Bháskaráchárjya. Even in this list we do not find any mention of the telescope. It was not known to the Mahomedan astronomers: "From the reign of the Abbassides," says Gibbon, "to that of the grand children of Tamarlane, the stars, without the aid of glasses, were diligently observed."‡

Mr. Colebrooke observes that the ancient Hindus were in considerable advance of their contemporaries in two points, one was in their

---

* *Asiatic Researches*: Translation of the *Zeej Mahomedshahy.*

† In his *Sacred City of the Hindoos, pp.* 136, 137.

‡ *The Decline and fall of the Roman Empire*, Ch. LII.

notions regarding the precession of the equinoxes, in which he says they were more correct than Ptolemy, and the other relates to the diurnal revolution of the earth round its axis,* not known to the world till the time of Copernicus. And with respect to the originality of the science among them, it cannot be denied, that at the time when they began to write treatises on astronomy, all other nations were in greater ignorance than they, and the principles which they deducted were not only peculiar and different from those of other nations, but shows "a knowledge of discoveries not made, even in Europe, till within the course of the last two centuries."†

In the *Súrya-siddhánta*, which is supposed to have been written in the fifth century of the Christian era, most of the calculations have been made with the aid of Trigonometry and Geometry. Both these sciences were therefore known to the Hindus long before the fifth century: for we should remember that these two systems could not be written in the infancy of science, the Hindus must have made very great

* Áryabhatta was the first and almost the sole astronomer who affirmed this theory: he was born in 476 A.D.; Copernicus was born in 1473 and died in 1543.

† Elphinstone's *History of India*, Book III, Ch. 1.

advancement in scientific knowledge before they could have undertaken to write on trigonometry and geometry. The *Súrya-siddhánta* contains "a system of Trigonometry, which not only goes far beyond anything known to the Greeks, but involves theorems which were not discovered in Europe till the sixteenth century." Bháskara also has given rules for the computation of sines in the *Siddhánta-siromani* entitled "The construction of the canon of sines."

Before the eighteenth century geometrical theorems were dispersed in the works of several writers on astronomy. The consequent inconvenience that was felt in imparting instruction on the subject and in calculations was removed by the illustrious Jayasinha* who caused a large volume to be compiled entitled *Kshetrádarsa* or a *View of Geometrical Knowledge*, comprising all that relate to the science. The demonstrations of the various properties of triangles and quadrilaterals found in the works of Bháskara and Brahmagupta, the theorems from which the area of the circle is computed and also the superficies and solidity of the cone and sphere, argue a very extensive knowledge of elementary

* *The Eleventh Discourse* of Sir William Jones.

geometry.* One of the most remarkable properties of triangles is that which expresses the area in terms of the three sides. It is given by Brahmagupta. "The proposition is, in reality, of no inconsiderable difficulty; and we confess," say a writer in the *Edinburgh Review*,† "that we did not expect to find it in the Geometry of Hindustan. We believe that it was unknown to the Greek geometers, and was, if we mistake not, first published by Clavius," in the sixteenth century. The knowledge of the proportion of the radius to the circumference of a circle, unknown to Europeans until modern times, was known, so far as can be traced, to the Hindu scientists of the fifth century.‡

The only book that is extant on the science of Arithmetic is the *Lilávati* of Bháskarácchárjya, but evidently the science was known to the Hindus from a very remote period, as a basis of all other sciences: either all the more ancient works on the subject are lost, or have become very rare. The *Lilávati* contains the common

---

* *Edinburgh Review*, Vol. XXIX, Art. VII.

† Ibid.

‡ The *Súrya-siddhánta* says "The diameter of the earth is 1600 *yoyanas*. Multiply the square of the diameter by 10, the square root of the product will be the circumference of the earth." Ch. 1, Sl. 59.

rules of the science, and "the application of those rules to a variety of questions on interest, barter, mixtures, combinations and permutations, the sums of progressions, indeterminate problems ; and lastly, the mensuration of surfaces and solids." The rules that relate to *supposition* (which according to English mathematicians is called False Position), Rule of Three, and combination exactly tally with those which are employed by the Europeans, yet nothing can be more independent than the conclusions of the Hindu mathematicians. "No demonstration nor reasoning, either analytical or synthetical, is subjoined, but on examination, the rules are not only found to be exact, but to be nearly as simple as they can be made, even in the present state of analytical investigation." But these defects are supplied by the commentators.* "The *Hindus*," says Sir William Jones, "are said to have boasted of *three* inventions, all of which, indeed, are admirable, the method of instructing by *apologues*, the *decimal scale* adopted now by all civilized nations, and the game of *chess*, on which they have some curious treatises."† And

* *Edinburgh Review*, Vol. XXIX, *Algebra and Arithmetic of the Hindus.*

† *The Third Anniversary Discourse : On the Hindu.*

they boasted justly, for owing to the invention of the decimal notation they had a decided advantage over the Greeks in the arithmetical science; it is no wonder therefore that the system should be adopted by the western nations, who could appreciate the convenience it affords for the purposes of calculation.

The Hindus attained a high degree of perfection in the science of Algebra. Bháskara gives us a separate treatise on it in the *Siddhánta-siromani*, called the *Vija-ganita*; and Brahmagupta also treats of it in the *Brahama-siddhánta*, another astronomical work. The former flourished, as we have already seen, in the twelfth century, and the date of the latter is fixed by Mr. Colebrooke in the sixth century of the Christian era. But both these writers are said to have derived their knowledge from the writings of A'rya Bhatta, which contain the refined artifice for the solution of indeterminate problems, known in Sanskrit by the name of *Cuttaca*. A'rya Bhatta is supposed by Mr. Colebrooke to have been the contemporary of the Grecian algebraist Diophantus, who lived in the fourth century before the Christian era at the time of the Emperor Julian. But the fact of the *Cuttaca* being found in the work of A'rya

Bhatta, not known to Diophantus, and the application of the truths of algebra to astronomy, supposes that both the sciences were in such a state of advancement, as the lapse of several ages and many repeated efforts of invention could only produce. In fact, Bháskaráchárjya cites not only Brahmagupta, but also Sridhar and Padmanábha, as the authors from whose voluminous works he acknowledges to have received his own materials.* But we do not know when these two last mentioned writers flourished. May they not have flourished before Árya Bhatta? However, the antiquity of Hindu algebra cannot be questioned.

Mr. Colebrooke institutes a comparison between the notation or algorithm of the Hindu algebraists with those of Greece and Arabia. "The Hindu algebraists use for their symbols abbreviations and initials of words: they distinguish negative quantities by a dot set over the letter or letters that denote the quantity; but they have no mark for a positive quantity, except the absence of the negative sign. They have no symbol that expresses addition, nor any

* *Vija-ganita*, Sl. 210.

ব্রহ্মাহ্বয় শ্রীধরপদ্মনাভবীজানি যস্মাদতিবিস্তৃতানি।
আদায় তৎসারমকারি নূনং সদ্যুক্তিযুক্তং লঘু শিষ্যতুষ্ট্যৈ॥

that either signifies equality, or the relation of greater or less. A product of two quantities is denoted by the initial syllable of the word *multiplication* subjoined to those quantities, or sometimes by a dot interposed between them...... Numeral co-efficients are employed including unity, and comprehending fractions, and are always written after the symbol of the unknown quantity."* "The notation which has just been described," says Mr. Colebrooke, "is essentially different from that of Diophantus, as well as from that of the Arabian algebraists, and their early disciples in Europe."† The Arabians do not use any symbol, but expresses everything by words at full length.

The algebra of the Hindus attained a high perfection on account of their knowledge of the *Cuttaca*, which is a general rule for the resolution of indeterminate problems of the first degree. It was not known in Europe till published by Bachet de Mezeriac about the year 1624.‡ But they had a decided superiority over the Greek algebraists in the excellence of their

* *Edinburgh Review*, Vol. XXIX.

† *Algebra with Arithmetic and Mensuration from the Sanskrit of Brahmagupta and Bháskara*, as quoted in the *Edinburgh Review*, Vol. XXIX.

‡ *Edinburgh Review*, Vol. XXIX, p. 151.

method and the perfection of their notation. The application of algebra to astronomical investigations and geometrical demonstrations is peculiarly a Hindu invention, and their manner of conducting it has been justly eulogized even in the present advanced condition of science.

This is a brief outline of some of the Hindu sciences. The more we know of these works, the more distinctly we can appreciate the genius of the Hindus and the extent of their investigations. Begging the pardon of Bently and Delambre, we humbly state that the antiquity of these Hindu sciences and their intrinsic merit, can only be ascertained when we, like Colebrooke, Davis, or Baillie, do not enter into investigation with the predetermined idea of disputing them. Mathematical science was in a state of perfection in the fifth century of the Christian era; but it could not have been so all on a sudden, and the books, that we at present possess, are in a fragmentary form which indicate them to be the relics of some remote period. The Hindus have no separate treatises on trigonometry, geometry, arithmetic and algebra, except those which are given by way of introduction to astronomy, not by all astronomers but only by a few. These sciences are made entirely subservient to that of astronomy, and as such their principles are dispersed in the several astronomical works, with only enunciations and examples not properly worked out. For the elementary parts, therefore, where the processes are given in full, the antiquarian should rake up the mouldering corners of a Bháskarácharjya's house. The history of algebra in the western countries leaves no doubt as to the originality of the Hindu science. "If the Greeks did not receive their first idea of algebra from the Hindus," says Professor Monier Williams,* "it may at least be taken as proved (from all that Colebrooke has so ably written on the subject), that the Hindus were certainly not indebted to the Greeks, but invented their system independently." The Khalif Almansur, who was a great patron of literature, caused "an Indian astronomical treatise" to be translated by the first Arabian mathematician. The Arabs themselves never think the science of algebra to be indigenous, but they humbly ascribe their knowledge to Diophantus of Alexandria.† It seems however that by the lapse of time, and owing to the

* *Indian Wisdom*, p. 184, note.

† Gibbon's *Decline and fall of the Roman Empire*, Vol. II, Ch. LII.

distance of the country, they had forgotten that the science was introduced among them from India. "The name algebra (from the Arabic *al jabr*, the reduction of parts to a whole or of fractions to integers) shows that Europe received algebra like the ten numerical symbols from the Hindus through the Arab."* Leonardo of Pisa first introduced Algebra into Europe at the beginning of the thirteenth century: he studied it at Bugia in Barbary.†

The decline of scientific knowledge among the Hindus does not date back from a remote period as is considered by many. The last of the annotations on scientific works, which are characterized by skill, acuteness, intelligence and judgment, is dated 1602 A.C.; it is very clear therefore that the light of science was shining in India at the distance of not less than three hundred years from the present period. The cause of this decay of scientific learning as well as that of the general prosperity of the Hindus lies imbedded in the history of the last thousand years. It did not happen all in a moment, but the cause must be looked for in the aggregate

* *Indian Wisdom*, p. 185.

† Elphinstone's *History of India*, Cowell's Edition, p. 145, note by the Editor.

influence of the results of manners, customs, habits and ideas of the time we are speaking of.

Musical science attained a very high refinement in ancient India. Such refinement bespeaks a nation peaceful, happy, and prosperous. No country can successfully cultivate the art if it be convulsed by internal commotions, or be in constant dread of external attack: it is purely an art of recreation. Though indeed we cannot fix the periods of Bharata, Hanumána, Dámodara Soma, Pavana, and Náráyana, writers on music, yet it cannot be doubted that the science and the art of music are of indigenous growth. The difference of the Hindu modes with those of other countries, the variations in the number of *srutis*, and the difference of the principles themselves, bear us out in our statement. "The Hindu system of music," says Sir William Jones, "has, I believe, been formed on truer principles than our own; and all the skill of the native composers is directed to the great object of their art, *the natural expression of strong passions*, to which melody, indeed, is often sacrificed: though some of their tunes are pleasing to an European ear."* India is a country of poetry and of feelings: it is no wonder therefore that music

* The *Third Anniversary Discourse*.

should be cultivated even from the earliest times. Musicians and dancers are mentioned in the Vedas* and in the Institutes of Manu. Old Nárada sang with his *Viná* in days of yore. The two sons of Ráma are mentioned in the *Rámáyana* to have been taught by Válmiki himself to sing the exploits of their father. The *Mahábhárata* speaks of songs and dances. Kátyáyana, the inventor of the *Viná* bearing his name, flourished at the time of Nanda, king of Magadha. The towns of Avanti and Alaká, as described in the *Meghaduta* of Kálidása, resounded to the sound of the *Mridanga*, the songs of the men, and the tinkling feet of the ballet-girls. The Gandharvas were a race of heavenly choristers, frequently spoken of in the earliest works; hence music itself was called *Gándharva-vidyá.* All this shows that the art was cultivated in all periods of ancient Hindu history.

The gamut of the Hindus is the same as that of the western countries, and it could not be otherwise; they reckon twenty-two *srutis* or quarters and thirds of a tone; and they use three *Saptakas* or heptachords. But the advancement of the Hindus in the science of music has been proved by the adaptation of the various

* Muir. J. R. A. S., *Atharva Veda*, VII, new series, Vol. II.

modes to different seasons and different parts of the day and night: each mode, again, has the power of exciting a particular sentiment or feeling. It is thus described: "Rága, which I translate a *mode*, may be according to *Soma* 960, but he selects from them as applicable to practice only twenty-three primary modes, from which he deduces many others. We have observed that eighty-four *modes*, or *manners*, might naturally be formed, by giving the lead to each of our twelve sounds, and varying in seven different ways, the position of the semitones."* Primary modes according to Pavana were arranged in the following manner according to the number of the Indian seasons:—

Sarat	... ...	Bhairava
Hemanta	... ...	Málava
Sisira	... ...	Sriirága
Vasanta	... ...	Hindola or Vasanta
Grishma	... ...	Dipaka
Varshá	... ...	Megha.

Each of these six *Rágas* or modes has got five, or according to others six, forms, called its *wives*, and they are known by the name of *Ráginis*. Each mode has three distinct sounds: "the note, called *graha*, is placed at the beginning, and that

* *Asiatic Researches*, Vol. III, *Music of the Hindus*.

named *nyása*, at the end, of a song: that note which displays the peculiar melody, and to which all the others are subordinate, that which is always of the greatest use, is like a sovereign, though a mere *ansa*, or portion. This clearly shows that the *ansa* must be the tonick, and we shall find that the other two notes are generally its third and fifth, or the mediant and dominant."*

Before the introduction of the musical instruments of the piano kind† in India, which have now greatly facilitated the learning of beginners, songs were, and are still now, learned by the vocal practice of sol-faing which gives a fixed tone and various evolutions to the voice, difficult to be achieved by means of those instruments. Hindu music is acknowledged by many Europeans to be "remarkably sweet," but to the ears of foreigners generally, it sounds dull and monotonous. There can be no doubt that music, like painting, requires cultivation of taste for its appreciation. Even the master-pieces of Raphael or Michael Angelo are unappreciated by the ignorant: the eye of a connoisseur at once detects the hand of a master in the lines of an ungaudy picture,

* *Asiatic Researches*, Vol. III.

† The Piano-forte was invented by Bartilommeo Christophali in Florence in 1710. See *Yantrakosha*, p. 48.

whereas the ignorant are taken by the brilliant colourings of a common dauber.

The country owes much to Raja Sourindra Mohun Tagore, not only for his patronizing the musical art, but also for the knowledge he disseminates in his valuable publications replete with laborious researches into the science of Hindu music. Among the ninety-nine instruments, which we use at present, a great number of them existed in ancient India. He assorts all these instruments into four classes: the stringed, the wind, the percussion, and the pulsatile instruments.* All these four classes were known to the ancient Hindus. The *mahati-viná* said to have been invented by Nárada, was in use in India before the lyre was known to the Greeks.† A considerable amount of knowledge is required to play upon it, which shows the progress made by the Hindus when the instrument was invented. In fact, Sonnerat and Fetis say that Europe, and other parts of Asia owe to India for their stringed instruments. The former considers them to be formed with modifications in the model of *Rávanástra*, an instrument made

* S. M. Tagore's *Yantrakosha*, and his *Short notice of the Hindu Musical instruments*, presented to the Indian Museum.

† *Yantrakosha*, p. 16.

by Rávana, king of Lanká; and the latter says "Hindoostan has, it appears, been the birth place of the instruments played with the bow, and has made them known to other parts of Asia. This does not admit of a moment's doubt, as the instruments are actually in existence, bearing unmistakeable mark of their Indian origin."* The *mridanga* a "drawing-room instrument" of the pulsatile class, is mentioned in the *Rámáyana*. The *dámámá*, the *panava*, the *dundhubhi*, and other instruments, mentioned in the *Rámáyana* and the *Mahábhárata*, were used in fields of battle. Ancient India owed to none for her music, it is here that the art has achieved its greatest triumph.

Though no ancient paintings have been transmitted to us yet it seems that at one time the Hindus attained a very high skill in the art. The frequent allusions in the Sanskrit dramatic works to portraiture of life and nature, leaves no doubt that the art was once successfully cultivated. It would have been really a study for the metaphysician to mark the different feelings through which Sitá successively passed when the associations of her life were vividly called forth by the picture which was placed before her by

* Quoted in the *Yantrakosha*, pp. 67 and 69.

her husband.* The portrait of Vatsarája is mentioned in the *Ratnávali* to have been drawn by Ságariká from memory, and yet it was so faithfully drawn that the king could at once recognise it as his own picture.† It evidently shows that the art must have made a very great advancement before ladies could have thought of learning it. In several other dramas we find also a female painter as one of the attendants of the heroine. The beautiful sculptural works in the cave-temples of southern India, show a knowledge of painting. But we can account for the non-existence of any picture of the period before the Mahomedan conquest. Time indeed has done her destructive work, but it is more to the ravages of invaders than to those of time that we ascribe this deprivation. If the ruthless hand of Lord Elgin in the nineteenth century could despoil Athens of some of her ancient monuments of art, it is not at all surprising that India's Mahomedan conquerors should feel no scruple for hers also. Mahmoud of Ghazni took away from India the gates of Somnath; Nadir of Persia her peacock-throne with the Koh-i-noor to boot, Ahmed Shah Abdalli her jewels and

---

* *Uttara Ramcharita*, Act 1, Scene II.

† *Ratnávali*, Act II.

ornaments. If every conqueror thus took away something that struck his fancy, there is scarcely any doubt that India was deprived of her ancient paintings.

Every nation must know more or less of medical science, but the attainment of a high skill depends upon the course of time, when by observations and experiments, the properties of natural objects and their effects upon the human body are ascertained. But this again varies according to the degree of attention that is paid to these subjects. The ancient Hindus were famous for their devotion to the useful arts of life: this important science, therefore, engaged their attention even at the earliest times. In the Riga-Veda the hygienic properties of some of the vegetables are mentioned; Soma was the deity of the medicinal herbs; and the Aswinis are called the physicians of the gods. The evidence of the practice of medicine can be had even during this period: "The carpenter seeks something that is broken, the doctor a patient;" in the same hymn it is said "I am a poet, my father is a doctor."* Physicians are mentioned in Manu, and the king is advised "to put in all things (edible) medicines which destroy

* Muir's *Riga-Veda*, IX, J. R. A. S. (new series) Vol. II, p. 28.

poison, and to wear always gems which are antidote to poison."* Such was the estimation in which the Hindus held the medical art, that they called forth into existence at the churning of the ocean, the story of which is given in the *Mahábhárata*, a physician named Dhanwantari along with ambrosia. He became the physician of the gods. In fact, in subsequent periods, *Dhanwantari* became a title of every distinguished physician. The second Dhanwantari is said to have been the author of the *Áyur-Veda*, or rather he revealed the science of medicine to his pupil, Susruta, as social laws and manners were revealed by Manu to Bhrigu; and the third, who flourished in the reign of Vikramáditya, became one of the nine "gems" of his court. Atreya wrote next, and his work, the *Atreya-Sanhitá*, is a compendium of the *Áyur-Veda*, as the author himself admits.† Charaka's *Sanhitá* is the next renowned work, which possesses greater interest than the *Áyur-Veda*, and shows the advancement made by the Hindus in medical science. Surgery is treated of in the work of Susruta, and the number of surgical

---

* *Manu*, Ch. III, 152; and Ch. VII, 218.

† Mrs. Manning's *Ancient and Mediæval India*, Vol. III, p. 340.

instruments used in ancient India, amounted, according to Dr. Royle, to one hundred and twenty-seven.

A detailed account of all these works is given in the volumes of Professor Wilson. According to him, the Hindus "attained as thorough a proficiency in medicine and surgery as any people whose acquisitions are recorded." They "define and distinguish symptoms with great accuracy, and their materia medica is most voluminous." Elphinstone, on the authority of Dr. Royle, says that "their acquintance with medicine seems to have been very extensive. We are not surprised at their knowledge of simples, in which they gave early lessons to Europe, and more recently taught us the benefit of smoking datura in asthma, and the use of cowitch against worms." "They were the first nation who used minerals internally."*

The Hindus had, at one time, attained a world-wide celebrity on account of their medical skill and medicines. Khalif Almansur caused some Hindu medical works to be translated from the Sanskrit into Arabian, among which we find "a tract upon poison by Shanak (meaning Charaka); and a treatise on medicine, or materia

* *History of India*, Book III, Ch. IV.

medica, by Shashurd (meaning Susruta)." One of the translators was named Gabriel Bactishna, a Syrian. Many celebrated Greek physicians were acquainted with the Hindu medical science, and they prescribed Hindu medicines: among these may be mentioned the names of Serapion, Actuarius, Avicenna, and Ætius, some of whom were the court physicians of the Khalif. Among the Hindu medicines which they often prescribed, or rather which we often meet with, may be mentioned the *triphalá** recommended by Charaka. Two Hindu physicians (both natives of India), named Manka and Saleh, lived in the court of Harun-al-Rashid.† The Arabs candidly acknowledge their obligations to the Hindus for their knowledge of the medical science. The Hindus had made so much advancement in the systems of pathology and therapeutics, that their observations could not have been possibly despised by any other nation who were acquainted with them.

In connection with this subject, we cannot

---

* It is a decoction of three fruits: *Haritaki* (Terminalia Chebula), *Bayará* (Terminalia Bellerica) and *Ámlaki* (Phyllanthus emblica).

† For a detailed account of the Greek physicians and their treatment by Hindu medicines, see Mrs. Manning's *Ancient and Mediæval India*, Vol. I, Ch. XVIII.

help adverting to the science of Botany. Botany has never been treated as an independent science except as an auxiliary to that of medicine. Though the Hindus have divided the vegetable kingdom into classes, order, genus, and species, yet the principles of Linnæus, or of Jussieu do not underlie their system, or rather their divisions have been made according to no principle, except a strong resemblance in external appearance. Yet their observations in this respect were vast and remarkable; and the descriptions, which they have given in their voluminous works* of trees, plants, shrubs, and fruits, are characterized by a minuteness and accuracy which can never mislead the reader: and their hygienic properties are described by Charaka and Susruta. Some of the names could not even now be recognized, some are becoming antiquated, and unless we take care to reduce them to their present nomenclatures, it would be impossible to identify them after three or four generations, and the sanatory effects of their properties would be positively lost to the world. An attempt at classification of the vegetable kingdom

* A medical gentleman of our acquaintance assured us that while he lived in Kashmir, he saw the manuscript of a Sanskrit Botanical work, consisting of three volumes, each of which is "as big as a Webster's Dictionary."

was made by Manu: "All vegetables grow either from seeds or from slips of branches; those are called *Aushadhi* (herbs) which having got fruits and flowers, perish when they ripe. Those are called *vanaspati* (lords of the forest) which having no flower produce fruits; those which get fruits from flowers, or fruits at once, are called *Briksha* (trees). There are *guchchhas* (shrubs) or those from the root of which stalks shoot up which are not stems, *gulmas* (reeds) with single roots producing shoots, these are of various sorts; *Trina* or grasses; climbers with tendrils are called *Pratána,* and *Balli* or creepers: these spring from seeds or slips or from both."* These stanzas also clearly show that propagation by cutting and layering was known to the Hindus at this period.

Their knowledge of Chemistry was very extensive. But like botany it is not treated as an independent science. The *Ayur-Veda* has a chapter on it; Charaka could not overlook the important science. Beside these, there are other books extant in India. The *Rasaratnákara,* the *Rasendra-chintámani* and others are compilations from ancient authors. "They knew how to prepare sulphuric acid, nitric acid, and

* *Manu,* Ch. I, Sls. 46 to 48.

muriatic acid; the oxide of copper, iron, lead (of which they had both the red oxide and litharge), tin and zinc; the sulphuret of iron, copper, mercury, antimony, and arsenic; the sulphate of copper, zinc, and iron; and carbonates of lead and iron. Their modes of preparing those substances seem, in some instances, if not in all, to have been peculiar to themselves."* The Indian dyes, which were so much prized in ancient Rome for their brilliancy and continuance of splendour, were evidently made by means of chemical process. The fluxing and compounding of metals, which were known to the ancient Hindus as we have already shown, could not have been made without the aid of chemistry. Though we have not, indeed, works on chemistry independent of the science of medicine, yet there is one great fact which cannot be overlooked: that the ancient Hindus knew more of this science than what they chose to disclose. The more we think of their battles, the more we read of their various sorts of arrows, the more confirmed we are in our belief that their chemical knowledge and skill were very great. We have already said that the arrowheads were coated with chemical properties. Again, when

* Elphinstone's History of India, Book III, Ch. IV.

we consider that they were never conquered by a foreign nation, till they had lost all knowledge of chemistry, as used in their ancient warfare, by a long continued enjoyment of peace, our opinion seems to become strengthened. Where was the necessity of going to a Brahmin for learning the military arts, if arrow-shooting depended entirely upon manual practice? The Brahmins, who were the receptacles of all knowledge, were frequently resorted to by the *kshatriya* class for learning their own profession. Sagara was taught by Aurba,* Ráma by Viswámitra, the Kurus and Pándavas by Drona, Karna by Parasuráma: all these were Brahmins, except Viswámitra who was a Kshatriya Brahminized. There would have been no cause for the heart-burning of Karna, had the shooting of arrows been merely a manual art, when Drona taught Aryuna more than him. In short, the *mantras* which these preceptors gave to

* In the preceding chapter (page 30) Aurba, the preceptor of Sagara, is said to be the inventor of the "fire" called *Aurbágni* (gunpowder), but it should be mentioned that the *Harivansa* (Chapter 45) ascribes the invention of the Aurbágni to Urba, the preceptor of the Asura Hiranyakasipu, and the "fire" is said to have been used by the Daityas in the battle between Indra and Maya Dánava. In the *Sukranitisára* (Chap. IV, Section 7, Slokas 201 and 202) by Sukrácharya the *Aurbágni* is called *Agnichurna.* The *Sukranitisára* describes the *Nálikástra* or the gun.

their respective pupils, were, we consider, nothing more than instructions in chemistry. It was therefore priestcraft which studiously concealed the sublime science of chemistry from the knowledge of the world. Publication of such knowledge would lessen that unbounded power which the priest-class wielded upon the rest of their countrymen. Even such men as the authors of the *Súrya-siddhánta* and the *Siddhánta-siromani*, who by their learning ought to have been exempt from such jealousies, published their knowledge of the astronomical instruments with a reluctance which is truly ridiculous. "The method (of constructing the revolving instrument)," says the author of the *Súrya-siddhánta*, "is to be kept a secret, as by its diffusion here it will be known to all (and there will be no surprise in it)."* "I have been induced," says the author of the *Siddhánta-siromani*, "to mention the construction of these (instruments) merely because they have been mentioned by former astronomers."† In fact, it is priestcraft which had to do with the downfall of India's prosperity.

Thus we have tried to show that the Hindu

---

* *Surya-siddhánta, Jyautishopanishat* Sl. 17, Sástri's Trans.
† *Siddhánta-siromani, Yantrádhdya*, Sl. 57, Wilkinson's trans.

sciences were the most ancient and original. In certain sciences their superiority was acknowledged by all ancient nations, in others, though they could not be placed foremost, yet they were second to none. India by her remarkable observations, skill, knowledge and genius, has done, directly or indirectly, an immense amount of good to the rest of the world.

CHAPTER III.

LITERATURE.

We have already said that the ancient Hindus were not the aborigines of India; they belonged to the Aryan race, and they were the last to migrate from their primeval abode. towards the south, whereas the previous migrations had been towards the west. It is said, the nations who spoke the Sanskrit, the Zend, the Greek, the Latin, the Slavonic, the Teutonic and the Celtic languages, originally sprung from a common stock, and spoke one common language. Their country was Ariana or modern Iran. Almost the whole of Europe and India were thus peopled by the Aryan race. It is inferred the same blood, flows through the veins of all these nations as a close affinity exists between their languages. The discovery of Sanskrit as the ancient language of India, first gave an impetus to the German School of philologers from the time of the Schlegels, and led to the deductions of those principles of philology which have been the basis of our knowledge regarding the history of pre-historic times and the relations of the several nations. Among the several languages which we have enumerated, the strongest and the closest affinities exist between the first four. Max Muller designates the Sanskrit the "eldest sister" of all the Aryan languages. "The Sanskrit language," says Sir William Jones, "is of a wonderful structure; more perfect than the Greek, more copious than the Latin, and more exquisitely refined than either."* Indeed, by the rules of compounds, suffixes, and inflexions, the Sanskrit language has become the most flexible, and there is no idea which cannot be expressed with ease and elegance by means of the various words which can thus be formed. Such was the language of ancient India: it is the key for unlocking the past, and by it many of the obscurities of the present may be illuminated. In short, we must depend upon Sanskrit literature alone for comprehending the state of Hindu society, both past and present, and for explaining those inconsistencies which seem to be inexplicable. It possesses a most comprehensive grammar† which

* *The Third Anniversary Discourse.*

† Among the several grammarians may be mentioned the name of Pánini, who, according to Professor Goldstucker, flourished in the sixth century before the Christian era at Salatura in the Gándhara country; Pánini himself mentions the names of Apisale, Kasyapa, Gargya, Gálava and other grammarians who preceded him; Kátyáyana who lived in the fifth

has never been equalled in perfection by that of any other language. It has also works* on rhetoric and rules of compositions, and lexicographies† which are written in such a style that they are committed to memory by every learned Hindu.

If dissemination of knowledge be a condition necessary, as it is, for the spread of civilization in a country, that condition was surely fulfilled by the ancient Hindus. Learning was enjoined upon the three upper-classes. To acquire knowledge formed part of a Hindu's duties: it was a means of obtaining beatitude in after-life. A Bráhman, whose special duty it was to impart and receive education, was an outcast from the "society of the virtuous" if he were devoid of any knowledge of the Vedas and the Sástras,

---

century B.C., Patanjali, contemporary of Pushpamitra, king of Pátaliputra, flourished in the second century, and Vopa Deva, who lived in the court of Hemádri, king of Devagiri (Dowlatabad).

* The principal works are the *Sáhityadarpana* by Vishwanath Kabirája, who is said to have lived in Dacca in the fifteenth century; the *Kávyadarsana* by Dandi; the *Kávyaprakása* by Mammata Bhatta, who being the maternal uncle of Sriharsa, author of the *Naishadha*, flourished in the eleventh century.

† There are numerous glossaries, among which may be mentioned the *Amarakosha* by Amarasinha, who lived in the sixth century; *Abhidhána-ratnamálá* by Haláyudha; the *Abhidhána-chintámani* by Hemachandra; and the *Medini*.

the injunctions of which he was to carry out in the routine of his daily life. He is to learn the three Vedas from his preceptor for a period of thirty-six years, or for half of that period, or till the end of his attainments.* The four sons of Dasaratha are said to have been learned in the Vedas though they belonged to the Kshatriya class.† The innumerable works that are still extant, notwithstanding the destruction of many by Mahmoud of Ghizni and other foreign invaders, attest the devotion of the ancient Hindus to learning and the promulgation of knowledge throughout the whole land. They embrace the entire results of thought ranging from the most abstruse notions of philosophy to the most comprehensive observations of nature. They include theology, metaphysics, science, polite literature, and their various expositions. They supply the desideratum of an actual written history by pointing out the march of Hindu ideas through the several stages of time.

No country in the world can boast of a work so ancient as the Vedas. They compose the whole groundwork of Hindu religion and litera-

---

* Manu, Chapter III, Sl. I.

† *Rámáyana*, *Bálakánda*, 18 *Swarga*, *Sl.* 25.

সর্ব্বে বেদবিদঃ শূরাঃ সর্ব্বে লোকহিতেরতাঃ ॥

ture. The word *Veda* means *Knowledge.* According to Hindu ideas, this knowledge emanated from the "Self-existent," and was heard by the Divine Spirits* of the Sun, Air and Fire, and by them it was communicated to the Rishis. Therefore the Veda is called *Sruti* or that which is heard, that is unwritten. When at last this knowledge, by continual growth, became too complex for oral transmission, it was reduced to writing by their pupils. These writings were afterwards collated and divided into separate volumes by Vyása. Manu, though he mentions the names of the four Vedas, Rig, Yayur, Sáma and Atharva, recognizes only the first three as authorities ;† but at the time of the *Rámáyana*, we see that all these four were equally regarded as infallible guides. Every Veda consists of two, or rather of three parts: *Mantra* or prayer embodied in metrical hymns ; *Brahmana* or ritualistic precepts and theological arguments written in prose. Some of these last are sometimes in a detached collection, which forms the third part called the *Upanishad* ; it is written in prose and occasionally in verses. The prayers

* सूक्ष्मरूपी as distinguished from स्थूलरूपी or what can be perceived by the senses.

† Manu, Chapter XI, Sls. 33 and 265.

and hymns are addressed to those phenomena of nature, which are the most grand and beautiful. They worshipped Dyaus (the sky), Prithivi (the earth), Mitra (the sun), Váyu (the air), Agni (the fire), and other physical forces before which all nations must naturally bow down, some in adoration and the more enlightened in awe and reverence. Of the relative greatness of all these powers the ancient Hindus had no fixed idea, but they worshipped in them that incomprehensible and indefinite Deity whose attributes were displayed by them. Commentators, in fact, define these terms as the several names of one God, Brahma.

Various sorts of metres are to be met with in Vaidic literature: the Gáyatri, the Trishtupa, the Jagati, and the Anushtupa metres are said to have issued from the mouth of the self-existent Deity.* India, we have said, is pre-eminently a country of poetry and feelings, caused evidently by those natural scenes which vary from the most sublime to the most beautiful. The ideas of the Hindus clothed themselves, naturally as it were, in the language of poetry.

Even in the earliest of the Vedas, the Rig Veda, we meet with graphic descriptions of

* *Vishnu Purána*, Part I, Chapter 5, Sls. 52-55

nature, abounding with striking thoughts and noble sentiments. The Brahmana portions "are really a series of rambling and unsystematic prose compositions intended to serve as ceremonial directories for the use of the priests in the exercise of their craft."*

Later as we come to the Institutes of Manu, a great difference in the language and idiom is perceptible. The code inculcates the pantheistic principles of the preceding age, but quite differently from the polytheism which the Hindu religion assumed at a much later period, both however are founded upon the same Sutras of Vaidic literature. It is a body of precepts and rules for the guidance of the several classes composing Hindu society. It is written in metrical verses like the other principal works of the Hindus. The code gives us a fine idea of the professions which each class followed in easy or straitened circumstances; it treats also of the social laws, manners and customs, the principles of polity, the nature of the administration of justice, the religious ceremonies, and the various rules for regulating a Bráhman's daily life, with penances for the expiation of sin. Manu's code is considered to be the oldest of all the Dharma-Sástras, which

* Prof. Monier Williams' *Indian Wisdom.*

are founded on the Grihya and Samayachareka Sutras of the later Vaidic literature. They prescribe rules for domestic rites and customs, and they are held in the highest esteem throughout all India.

After the Institutes of Manu, the works which afford us a knowledge of ancient Hindu manners and customs, are the two great epics of India, the *Rámáyana* and the *Mahábhárata*. Much discussion has indeed been raised regarding the comparative ages of the poems; we, however, cannot but give the *Rámáyana* precedence in point of time. At the time of Válmiki, that portion of India was only populated and civilized, which was known by the name of Áryávartta, that is the country lying between the Himalaya and the Vindhya ranges, while the south was covered with deep forest and lived in by wild beasts and still wilder aborigines. At the time of Vyása, we see almost the whole of India teeming with Aryan population, and the celebrated Dandakáranya, the name of which is not even mentioned in the *Mahábhárata*, was no longer an *Aranya* or forest, but it bristled with innumerable houses inhabited by people who were far in advance in civilization over those described in the *Rámáyana*. In the latter the simplicity of an ancient people is described, whereas in the *Mahábhárata* we have the picture of a people lolling in luxury. The growth of population and luxury is the result of time. The practice of Sati was unknown at the time of the *Rámáyana*, but in the *Mahábhárata* a few instances occur, showing that the custom was only beginning to be known during that period. The comparative simplicity of the style of the *Rámáyana* supports also the view that it was written long before the *Mahábhárata*.

As the stories of the two epics are well known by the publications of the originals and their translations, we are not required to give a detailed account of them. The *Rámáyana* gives the history of Ráma, son of Dasaratha, king of Ajodhyá, and his war with Rávana, king of Lanká, for the recovery of his wife whom the latter had carried away from the forest of Dandaka, where she was residing with her husband and his brother, who had gone there to fulfill the vows of their father. The *Mahábhárata* gives the history of the sons of Pándu and their wars with the Kurus, the sons of Dhritaráshtra, for the recovery of their rightful dominion over the kingdom of Hastinápur.

Previous to the invention of the art of

printing, no ancient work, which had a strong hold on the popular mind, can be said to have been devoid of interpolations and variations. It is either a morbid love of fame of the interpolators to see their own compositions passed as the productions of the immortal authors, or a desire to claim for the clan to which they belonged a descent from the gods, or the false vanity of seeing their own principles inculcated as if cherished by the authors themselves, that caused these foistings and tamperings with popular works. The introductory chapters of the first book of the *Rámáyana*, giving a summary of the plot, the passages identifying Ráma with the Supreme Deity, the episode of Gangá, many passages regarding the doctrines of Chárváka and Buddha, and the whole of the seventh book, are considered by critics to be modern appendages. Genuine manuscripts of the *Rámáyana* have become very scarce.* The principal story of the *Mahábhárata* cannot occupy more than a fifth of the whole work, but so many additions and interlacings have been subsequently made, that the original form can not be clearly recognized. It has passed through

* We have heard that a true copy of the *Rámáyana* can be had at Mathura.

several stages of construction and reconstruction for centuries, until arranged and reduced to its present shape.* These two works are the inexhaustible source from which writers of subsequent periods have drawn their inspiration. They have supplied them with necessary materials, with which, by the aid of their genius, they have constructed their monuments of fame. In spite of the many interpolations, inconsistencies and anachronisms, they are read by every class of people with avidity as the productions of authors whom they invest with the divine spirit.

The subsequent literature of India is divided into two parts, according to what is *heard* and what is *seen*. The former again is divided into three classes according to style: (1) Poetry, (2) Prose, and (3) Poetry and prose mixed. (1) Poetical literature is divided into three parts: Mahá-Kávya or great poems, Khanda-Kávya or Lyrics, and Kosha-Kávya or collection of stanzas without connection except of the principal sentiment. (2) Prose literature is divided into stories and apologues. (3) Those which are written in poetry and prose are called Champu-Kávyas.

* Profs. Lassen and Monier Williams: See. *Indian Wisdom*, p. 372.

The latter division, or what is seen, consists of dramas, which are again divided into Rupakas and Upa-rupakas, the former being of ten species and the latter eighteen.*

A Mahá-Kávya is defined in the *Sáhitya Darpana* as the narrative of a god, or a noble-born Kshatriya, firm and high-spirited, or of many kings of the same line of descent, or of many families; it should be divided into *swargas* or cantos not less than eighteen; different metres should be employed; at the end of each canto suggestion should be made of what is to follow in the next. One principal feeling *(Rasa)*, either the erotic *(Sringára)* or heroic *(Vira)* should pervade the whole poem, though off and on other sentiments could be employed to enliven the imagery.

The *Raghu-Vansa* of Kálidása is the best of all the Mahá-Kávyas that are now extant.† But it is a matter of regret that we know nothing of this great poet of world-wide celebrity, except that he was one of the nine gems of the court of Vikramáditya, and that he was the author of the *Raghu-Vansa*, *Kumára-*

* *Sáhitya-Darpana*, Ch. IV.

† In treating of the literature of this period we have followed the excellent method adopted by Issur Chunder Vidyáságara in his *Discourse on the Sanskrit Language and Literature.*

Sambhava, *Meghaduta*, *Sakuntalá* and other poems. In fact the biographies of all the famous poets of India are mere matters of conjecture and inference. The *Bhoja-Prabandha* says that he was one of the poets of the court of Bhoja. But there were more than twelve Bhojas, and not less than eight Vikramádityas, and more than three Kálidásas we are aware of: one as the author of the *Sakuntalá*, another as the author of the *Nalodaya*, and the third, the author of *Jyotirvidabharana*, who tries to identify himself with the author of the *Raghu-Vansa*. Thus great confusion arises regarding the identification of Kálidása and the time in which he lived. Professor Lassen and others place him in the middle of the third century A.C., Elphinstone assigns him the fifth century, but Dr. Bhau Daji and Professor Weber fix his period in the sixth century, which is the probable age in which he lived, inasmuch as it is well known that he was the contemporary of Varáha Mihira and Amara Sinha.* The date of Varáha Mihira has been fixed by Sir William

* ধন্বন্তরি ক্ষপণকামরসিংহ শঙ্কু
বেতালভট্ট ঘটকর্পর কালিদাসাঃ।
খ্যাতো বরাহমিহিরোনৃপতেঃ সভায়াং
রত্নানি বৈ বররুচির্নব বিক্রমস্য॥

Jones at the beginning of the sixth century,* and the date of Amarasinha has also been fixed by Cunningham in the sixth century.†

Kalidása was a poet not of India only, but of all countries. Whoever reads his works, whether he be a foreigner or a native, is charmed by his faithful delineations of nature, his striking imagery, his minute descriptions of the workings of passion, especially of the sentiment of love, his exquisite fancy and taste, and the easy flow of his language, devoid of any forced construction or redundancy. His similies are apt and all drawn from natural objects, and in this respect he stands unrivalled among the poets either of India or of any other country. He was truly the favourite son of nature. With Kálidása alone for their poet, the Hindus can vie with the poets of any other country in the field of literature. Almost all his works have been translated into most of the European languages. All his works display transcendental genius. The *Raghu-Vansa* is divided into nineteen cantos. It contains the history of the princes of the Solar line from Dilipa to Agnivarna, the twenty-fourth in descent from Ráma. Every portion of

---

* *Asiatic Researches*, Vol. II.

† *Archælogical Survey Report* for 1861-62.

the work testifies to the extraordinary genius of Kálidása. His *Kumára-Sambhava* is another poem which belongs to the class of Mahá-Kávyas. It describes the love of Párvati and Siva, their espousal, the birth of Kumára or Kárttika, and his destruction of Táraka, an Asura, who had oppressed the gods and driven away Indra from the throne of heaven. It is divided into seventeen cantos, of which seven are generally read; and the last ten cantos, on account of the many improper descriptions, which they contain, of the love of the divinities, Párvati and Siva, as if they were beings of the terrestrial sphere, were rarely read and consequently remained unpublished. The ten cantos, however, have now been published by Pandit Tárá Náth Tarkaváchaspati from a Dravidian manuscript.

Among the six great *Mahá-Kávyas* which are generally read, the four others are the *Bhatti-Kávya* by Bhatta, the *Kirátárjuniya* by Bháravi, the *Sisupálabadha* by Mágha, and the *Naishadhacharita* by Sriharsha.

The subject of the *Bhatti-Kávya* is taken from the *Rámáyana*. It is divided into twenty-two cantos. Though it was purposely composed for the practical illustration of grammar, and consequently contains a great variety of diction an figures of poetry and rhetoric as may conveniently serve the object, yet its style is neither obscure nor inelegant; nor is it wanting in those poetical descriptions and true descriptions of nature which may rank it among the great poems of the country. Its authorship however is ascribed by some to *Bhartrihari* and by others to *Bhatta*. We of course side with the latter, as the author himself says that he wrote it during the reign of Sridharasena, king of Valabhipura,* who, according to Professor Lassen, reigned from 530 to 544 A. C. Bhartrihari was the reputed brother of Vikramáditya, and was for sometime king of Ujjaini, who, of course, could not have written it under the patronage of another king.

From the style of composition of the *Kirátárjuniya*, Bháravi is considered by Vidyáságara and others to have lived long before Mágha and Sriharsha. The poem, according to merit, may be placed next to the works of Kálidása. The subject is the asceticism of Arjuna, one of the five Pándavas, his fight with Siva, who came to him disguised as the king of the Kirátas, an

---

* কাব্যমিদং বিহিতং ময়া বলভ্যাং
শ্রীধরসেননরেন্দ্রপালিতায়াম্ ।
কীর্ত্তিরত ভবতান্নৃপস্য তস্য
ক্ষেমকরঃ ক্ষিতিপো যত প্রজানাম্ ॥

aboriginal tribe of India. Siva was much satisfied with his heroism and skill in archery, and taught him the knowledge of the bow, by means of which Arjuna became the first great warrior of his time. The poem is divided into seventeen cantos. Though much inferior to Kálidása, yet Bháravi was one of the great poets of India, and his poem abounds with instances of extraordinary genius.

The *Sisupálabadha* of Mágha and the *Naishadha* of Sriharsha show more of artistic ingenuity than poetical talent. The subjects of both the poems are taken from the *Mahábhárata*. The former relates the history of the conflict between Krishna and Sisupála, king of Chedi, in which the latter was slain. The cause of the dispute was Yudhishthira's giving divine honours to Krishna, which excited the envy of the king of Chedi, who thought himself not only equal, but in some respects superior, to the former. The greater portion of the poem is taken up with irrelevant matter, and the author frequently digresses from the main subject. The *Naishadhacharita* gives the history of Nala, king Nishadha, up to the time of his marriage. Sriharsha was also the author of *Khandana-khanda-khádya* and other works, but he should not be confounded with the author of the *Ratnávali.* Sriharsha, the author of *Naishadha,* was one of the five Brahmins who were brought by A'disura from Kányakubja to Bengal,* and he therefore flourished at the beginning of the eleventh century. The style of the *Naishadha* is harsh and inelegant, and greatly laboured.

Both the *Sisupálabadha* and the *Naishadha,* however, are not, wanting in passages of true poetic feeling, in just delineation and in noble sentiments. But in both of them perspicuity is sacrificed to the love of alliteration; and the perverted taste of the Bráhmans, according to whose idea every work which with difficulty could be understood was the best, placed them in the foremost rank in consideration of their merit,† over-riding the claims of Kalidása.

But Sriharsha, Mágha, Bháravi and Bhatt

---

* ভট্টনারায়ণো দক্ষোবেদগর্ভোহথ চান্দড়ঃ।
অথ শ্রীহর্ষ নামাচ কান্যকুব্জাৎ সমাগতাঃ॥

† With respect to the *Sisupálabadha* :—
উপমা কালিদাসস্ত ভারবেরর্থগৌরবম্।
নৈষধেঃ পদলালিত্যং মাঘে সন্তি ত্রয়ো গুণাঃ॥

and again
পুষ্পেষু জাতী নগরেষু কাঞ্চী নারীষু রম্ভা পুরুষেষু বিষ্ণু।
নদীষু গঙ্গা নৃপতৌ চ রামঃ কাব্যেষু মাঘঃ কবি কালিদাসঃ॥

With respect to the *Naishadha*
উদিতে নৈষধে কাব্যে ক মাঘঃ ক চ ভারবিঃ।

were thorough masters of the language; and in their hands, the flexibility of the Sanskrit, its adaptability to different sorts of style from the most diffuse to the most concise, its power of forming compounds, its various sorts of metre, the different meanings of its words which can be easily made to slide into puns and alliterations, and other capabilities of the language, are shown to the fullest advantage; and, according to the testimony of eminent linguists, "there is nothing in the whole range of Greek or Latin or any other literature that can be compared with these poems."*

Besides these there are the *Rághavapándaviya* by Kavirája, and other poems which come under the classification of *Mahá-Kávyas.*

Khanda-Kávyas are short poems written in the manner of *Mahá-Kávyas,* though not often divided into cantos. Among them Kalidása's *Meghaduta* is the best. In this charming little poem the reader is transported, as it were, to a place where all is lovely, good and pleasing. Though its language is comparatively more difficult than that of his other works, yet it is flowing and it sounds like music to the ear of the reader. The graphic but faithful descriptions

---

Indiau Wisdom, Sec. XV.

of natural scenery, the beautiful imagery that is raised up at every step, the description of the softer feelings of the heart, the delicacy of thought, and the fine taste,—all of which are to be found in this work,—have made it like a garland where all the sweetest and loveliest flowers are joined together. Had all the other works of Kálidása perished, this little book alone would have been sufficient to place his name among the immortal bards. The story is a simple one: a Yaksha, one of the servants of Kuvera, was exiled by his master to Rámagiri, near Nagpur, where feeling much for the separation from his wife, he asks a cloud to be his messenger, and directs its passage from that place to his abode at Alaka in the Himalaya, and describes to it his own feelings.

The *Ritusanhára* is another lyrical poem of Kálidása much admired by Sanskrit scholars. It describes the six seasons in six cantos. The *Nalodaya* is another *Khand-Kávya*, the authorship of which is ascribed by some to Kálidása, the author of the *Raghu-Vansa*, and by others to Kálidása, a poet of the court of Rájá Bhoja, who reigned at Dhar in the sixth century. There are many other works extant in Sanskrit which belong to this class.

The *Niti-sringára* and *Vairágya-sataka* of Bhartrihari, the *Sánti-sataka* of Silhana, the *Drishtánta-sataka* of Kusumadeva, and many others belong to the class of *Kosha-Kávya*, of which *Amaru-sataka* is the best. We have scarcely any time to notice all these minor poems, but many of these are published in a collected form in a work called the *Kávya-sangraha.*

Prose works, comparatively speaking, are few in Sanskrit literature: the *Kádamvari* by Bánabhatta, the *Dasakumára-charita* by Dandin and the *Vásavadattá* by Subandhu, are the principal prose works which are generally read, and they are classified under the general name of *Kávya* as they possess all the qualities of a poem, except the metrical language. Subandhu's work is the oldest, as he was the nephew of Vararuchi, one of the nine gems of the court of Vikramáditya, and Subandhu wrote his *Vásava dattá*, just after the death of that king: he therefore must have lived in the latter end of the sixth century. But superior merit is justly allowed to the *Kádamvari:* it is characterized by minuteness of description and by poetical thoughts, and though the general style is elegant, yet in some portions it has become harsh owing to the author's attempt to pander to the bad taste of the time by the use of alliterations, large compounds, and words conveying a double sense. Bána lived in the court of Harsha-Vardhana or Siláditya of Kanouj in the seventh century. He was the contemporary of Mayura Bhatta, the author of the *Súrya-sataka.* He is said to have been patronized by Vriddha Bhoja, who lived in the latter end of the sixth century, and it is perhaps after the death of that prince that he lived in Kanouj. Dandin, the author of *Dasakumára-charita*, lived in the eleventh century at Pátaliputra.

Among fables are to be mentioned the *Vetála-panchavinsati*, the *Singhásana-dvátrinsat*, the *Suka-saptati* which has been translated into the Persian under the name of *Tutinámá*, and the *Vrihat-kathá*, of which the *Kathá-sarit-ságara* is a compendium written by Somadeva in the middle of the twelfth century.

The original invention of apologues is claimed by the Hindus. The earliest work extant is the *Panchatantra* by Vishnu Sarman, who is also the author of the *Hitopadesa*, another work of a similar nature. The *Panchatantra* has been translated into almost all the languages of Europe and Asia; it has been thought that the

Greek Æsop and the Arabian Lokman owed much to the Hindus.* It is divided into five *Tantras* or chapters; and it teaches domestic, social and political duties by means of fables, in which animals figure as speakers.

The *Champu-Kávyas* are written in prose and poetry. Vidyáságara says that among the works which he has seen, the *Aniruddha-Charita* by Devarája is the best: but none of them in his opinion deserves any special eulogy.†

The *Drisya-Kávyas*, or those poems which are to be seen or rather seen and heard, consist of dramatic compositions. No department of literature can give a picture of real life in its true colours, with the manners, customs, feelings and prejudices of the people, as the drama. The drama of ancient India is the best portion of Sanskrit literature. It is like her arts, sciences,

---

* *Indian Wisdom*, pp. 508, 509. The *Panchatantra* was translated into Pahlavi in the reign of Nushervan about 570 A.C. and was known by the name of *Fables of Bidpai* or *Pilpay*; into Arabic in the reign of Khalif Almansur about 760 A.C., and was called *Kalila wa Damna*; into Hebrew by Rabbi Joel in the 15th century; into Persian in the 15th century; into Latin by John of Capua at the end of the 15th century; and from the latter into Italian, Spanish, and German. The Turkish translation was made in the reign of Sulaiman I, and was called Humayun Nama. The English translation was made from the French (Professor Monier Williams).

† *Discourse on the Sanskrit Language and Literature.*

epics and philosophy, perfectly original. The Greeks and the Chinese have dramatic compositions, but the difference of the Hindu system from that of each of those two nations, confirms its original character.* European dramatic literature does not date back beyond the fifteenth century, when the Hindu drama was in its decline. We have a play which is traced to the beginning of the Christian era. But the Hindus themselves ascribe their knowledge of theatrical representations to Bharata, a Rishi who was inspired by Brahmá and who taught the heavenly choristers, the *Apsarás* and the *Gandharvas*, in the musical art with its appurtenances of *nritta* (dance) and *nátya* (drama). Though no work of Bharata is extant, yet extracts from his work are quoted in the *Dasa-rupaka* and in the commentaries of the plays. Dramatical performances are said to have been made at the time of Asoka, the celebrated Buddhist monarch, who reigned in Magadha in the third century before the Christian era.

The Hindus had no regard for the unities of time, place and action, and their plays, it seems, were performed but once on some day of reli-

* Wilson's *Theatre of the Hindus*: Preface, p. XII.

gious festival or other merry occasion, but no particular season was fixed for scenic entertainments. The greater portion of a play is written in Sanskrit, the *Prákrita* language only being used when women, children, and low class people are the speakers. As all the plays that are now extant were written from the beginning of the Christian era, when Sanskrit had altogether ceased to be the vernacular of India, which may be proved from the language of the edicts of Asoka, it is plain these plays were intended for the learned few. Professor Wilson considers that these entertainments were given at the houses of great men, where a particular apartment was set apart for singing and dancing called the "*Sangitsálá*"* or more appropriately the *Nátyasálá.*

The Hindus are a soft-hearted people who do not wish to torture the mind. Therefore it is that they have got no tragedy in their dramatic literature. Whatever may be the plight of the hero or heroine when the incident is being developed, the author as a rule must bring the play to a happy termination, so that the audience does not go away with a heavy heart mourning over the fortunes of the principal characters

* *Theatre of the Hindus:* Preface, p. LXIV.

with whom their interest is bound up when the play is enacted.

In some of the plays the conduct of the plot is so dexterously managed, the incidents are so ingeniously connected and brought about, the characters are so skilfully delineated, and the works themselves are written in such happy and bold language, that their authorship even if ascribed to the greatest writers of Europe would not at all detract from the fame they have achieved. In the management of the stage, in the stage-directions and in various scenic artifices, the ancient Hindu dramas resemble the modern dramas of Europe.

Every play opens with a *nándi* or prayer in which the blessing of some deity is invoked upon the audience. Then follows a dialogue between the manager and one or two actors, or between the manager and his wife, in which an account is given of the author of the play, and reference is made to past occurrences as may be necessary for the understanding of the plot. At the end of the discourse, which is called the *prastábaná* or prologue, the manager by some exclamation adroitly introduces the *dramatis personæ*, and thus the play commences, which is divided into acts and scenes.

There are altogether the names of eighty-two Sanskrit plays of which only thirty-three are extant, the names of the rest are to be found in the various rhetorical works.*

A hundred years ago the whole of the literary world of Europe was surprised by the publication of the translation of *Sakuntalá* by Sir William Jones. An incitement was given to research into the literary lore of ancient India. The English translation of Sir William Jones was translated into German. Men of acknowledged genius like Goethe, Schlegel and Humboldt lavished eulogies upon *Sakuntalá*: they could discern the merits of the original work even through the hazy light of the translation of a translated work. What could be more gratifying to national pride than to hear such praise from Goethe himself, a foreigner:—

> Wouldst thou the young year's blossoms and the fruits of its decline,
> And all by which the soul is charmed, enraptured, feasted, fed?
> Wouldst thou the earth and heaven itself in one sole name combine?
> I name thee, O Sakuntalā! and all at once is said.†

Sir William Jones calls Kálidása, the author of the play, the "Shakespeare of India," and he

---

* Vidyáságara's *Discourse on the Sanskrit Language and Literature*, p. 74.

† Mr. E. B. Eastwick's translation as quoted by Prof. Monier Williams.

quotes a native epigram in his praise: "Poetry was the sportful daughter of Válmiki, and having been educated by Vyása, she chose Kálidása for her bridegroom after the manner of Vidharbha: she was now old and decrepit, her beauty faded, and her unadorned feet slipping as she walks: in whose cottage does she disdain to take shelter?" The work has since been translated into almost all the languages of Europe.

The subject is taken from the *Mahábhárata*: it describes the love of Dushmanta and Sakuntalá, their clandestine marriage, the desertion of the latter by her husband under circumstances over which he had no control, and her subsequent restoration. It breathes poetry in every passage: the work is a picture of human nature under certain circumstances, the description of the sentiment of love being the especial forte of the author. The beauty of the work can better be felt than described: to point out any particular passage as being stamped with the genius of the author is to quote the whole work itself.

Two other works, the *Vikrama-urvasi* and the *Málavikágnimitra*, are ascribed to Kálidása; the former though much inferior to *Sakuntalá* is not, however, unworthy of the author of

Sakuntalá; the latter is said to have been written during his earlier years.

Of all the plays that are now extant, the *Mrichchhakatika* is the oldest. It is ascribed to king Sudraka who is said to have lived long before Vikramáditya, and is mentioned in the *Vishnu Purána* and other works. If the latter be the starter of the Samvat era, then Sudraka must have lived in the second century before the Christian era, and not in the second century *after* the Christian era, as is said by some. There are many works which are ascribed to royal authors: but it is not at all likely that this play could have been written by Sudraka himself, because he says that he burnt himself to death after living for one hundred years and ten days, and he describes his personal appearance in the prelude. There are indeed Hindu authors who, like Jayadeva and Bhavabhuti, were conscious of their own merits, yet the description of one's personal appearance is very singular. It was evidently written by a poet of his court after his death, who dedicated the work to his memory. A revolution in the government of Oujein forms the underplot of the play. It gives a lively picture of the manners and habits of the people, and shows a state of society sufficiently advanced in civilization as to become luxurious and loose in morals. Intrinsic evidence also establishes the antiquity of the play, for therein we see many customs in vogue which have since fallen into disuse.

Bhavabhuti was the next great poet after Kálidása in point of merit as well as time. He was born at Padmapura in Berar, and he lived in the court of Yasovarmana who reigned at Kanouj in the eighth century. Three plays were written by him: the *Mahá-viracharita*, the *Uttaracharita*, and the *Málatimádhaba*. The *Mahá-viracharita* gives the history of Ráma to the time of his return from Lanká after the recovery of his wife; the *Uttaracharita* is a continuation of the story of Ráma from the time of his becoming king of Ajodhya. The former excels in heroic sentiments and feelings, and the latter is full of pathos. The story of *Málatimádhava* was not taken from any existing work, but is a pure invention of the author. It describes the love of the hero and heroine whose names give name to the play. Bhavabhuti possessed a very great power of describing natural scenery: he delineates nature in all her magnificence and grandeur; and though the stories of his first two plays were taken from the *Rámáyana*, yet he had skill in taking away the tedium of a twice-told tale by placing it in a new light before his readers.

The *Ratnávali* is a celebrated play, the prologue of which says that it was written by king Sriharsha, who reigned in Kashmir in the twelfth century, but there are many writers who, on the authority of the *Kávyaprakása*, a rhetorical work, consider that it was written by Dhávaka. Sriharsha is represented by Kalhana, the author of the *Rájatarangini*, as a great patron of literature, and himself a poet and versed in many languages.* The *Nagánanda* is another play which is ascribed to Sriharsha.

The *Mudrá-Rákshasa* is perhaps the only work which is purely of a political character. It describes the Machiavelian policy of Chánakya, one of the greatest politicians India ever produced. Chánakya murdered Nanda, king of Pátaliputra, in order to avenge a personal insult, and placed Chandragupta on the throne. Chánakya was fully aware that the Maurya

* *Rájatarangini*, *Taranga* VII, Sl. 611. Professor Wilson supposes that the author of the *Ratnávali* was Sriharsha, king of Kásmir, but it is now settled that either Bánabhatta or Dhávaka of the court of Sriharsha (or Siláditya II) who reigned at Kánouj in the seventh century, was the real author of the work. Sriharsha of Kánouj was visited by Hiuen Tsiang in 636 A.D.

prince, his protégé, would not be firm on the throne of Magadha, unless he was assisted in the affairs of the state by the able advice of Rákshasa, one of the most faithful ministers of Nanda; the object of the play is to bring about a reconciliation of Rákshasa with Chandragupta.

The *Prabodha-Chandrodaya* by Krishna Misra, who flourished in the twelfth century, is a play of a very different character. It resembles the *Moralities* of the middle ages, where metaphysical faculties are brought forward as *dramatis personæ.*

These are the most celebrated works which are generally read. It will be seen from the works extant that Hindu literature had its highest development during one thousand years of the Christian era, when along with intellectual progress, their manners and habits, underwent a great change.

CHAPTER IV.

PHILOSOPHY AND RELIGION.

Poetry is the mother of philosophy. Nowhere has this theory been so finely illustrated as in India and in Greece. The Orphic poems, and to some extent the poetry of Homer and Hesiod, paved the way for those philosophical enquiries for which Greece became afterwards so celebrated. In India the meditations of nature, which were poured forth in poetical effusions in the hymns of the Vedas, led to the inquiry into the nature of the soul and of the material world, and of the relation that subsists between them and the Creator. The mind of man cannot long remain satisfied with the mere contemplation and recital of the glory, wisdom, and power of God, but must soar up to those abstruse thoughts where a solution of the relation of the Creator and the created can be obtained. Thus the *Upanishads* came into existence, containing those germs of philosophical enquiries which were afterwards developed by later writers. Though much later in point of time to the *Mantras* and the *Brahmanas*, the Upanishads form a part of the Vedas, revealed and unwritten. Max Muller calls this period an epoch of the human mind. Whatever might have been the tendency of individual philosophers, whether their doctrine was atheistical or otherwise, all Hindu philosophy respects the authority of the Vedas, otherwise they would not have been read by any person professing the Hindu religion.

There are six systems of philosophy. It is impossible to ascertain their precise periods or their comparative ages. There can be no doubt, however, that these systems were elaborated after long intervals of each other: philosophers, unlike religious reformers, do not represent the consciousness of the time in which they live, but they soar above popular ideas through the power of independent thought, giving them a new tendency and direction, and thereby shape the course of the national intellect: a long period must necessarily elapse before the advent of another genius to give a new turn to ideas. But it is certain that all these systems were completed before Buddha began to preach his social and ethical doctrines in the sixth century before the Christian era. The six systems of Hindu philosophy are the *Vedánta* founded by Vyása, the *Mimánsá* by Jaimini, the *Sánkhya* by

Kapila, the *Yoga* by Patanjali, the *Nyáya* by Gotama, and the *Vaiseshika* by Kanáda.

The Hindu philosophical doctrines are perfectly original. They bear a strong resemblance to those of the Grecian schools. The *Vedánta* offers many parallels to the idealism of Plato, the *Vaiseshika* to the Atomistic system, the *Sánkhya* has been compared partly with the metaphysics of Pythagoras, the *Yoga* partly with that of Zeno, and the *Nyáya* has many things in common with the practical philosophy of Aristotle. There are some scholars who assert, rightly or wrongly, that many of the Greek doctrines have been taken from India, but none avers that India is indebted to Greece for any of her theories. Pythagoras is said to have travelled to India, and derived his doctrine of the metempsychosis from this country; Democritus of Abdera, one of the founders of the Atomistic school, is also said to have travelled to Egypt and India; and Gladisch asserts that the doctrine of the Eleatics is the regeneration of Hindu consciousness.* The object of all these systems is to teach mankind the way to *Mukti* or deliverance from the ills of life.

* Dr. Ueberweg's *History of Philosophy*, Vol. I.

The *Vedánta Sutras*, or aphorisms, are ascribed to Vyása or Bádaráyana, the compiler of the Vedas; but at this distant period, it is impossible to say whether the identification is correct. Of the six systems, the *Vedánta* is the most orthodox, being founded upon the Vedas and Upanishads. It propounds the pantheistic doctrines of the latter. Brahma or God is omniscient and omnipotent; he is the cause of the production and existence of the universe. He is the *Paramátmana* or universal soul, all individual souls (*Jivátmana*) are of his substance. The latter, therefore are immortal. Dissolution is absorption in his substance. He is the pervading spirit, therefore there is no material world as distinct from him. The true knowledge of a substance is to know it in reality; it does not depend on a man's notions. The true knowledge of Brahma therefore is not what we think of him. By this knowledge a man attains the highest object, *i. e.*, *parama purushártham* or salvation. Though Brahma is pure and rational, yet the inequalities of the world are accounted for by his dependence for creation on merit and demerit. The world is considered by the old Vedantists to be without beginning there were no inequalities at first, but merit and demerit being dependent on actions, such inequalities occurred afterwards. According to the later Vedantists the world is all *Máyá* or illusion; and they account for the inequalities of the world by calling into existence *Avidyá* or false knowledge as the creator of the external world and of individual souls. By reason of this power the individual soul regards the world, its own body and mind as real; but in truth they are not realities, just as the rope which is mistaken in the dark for a snake is not a real snake. There is nothing which really exists, except Brahma.

The whole object of the Vedánta is the identification of God and the human soul; their relation is that of pure identity; it is ignorance which produces the notion of duality, or which makes us believe in man's separate existence; the end of knowledge therefore is the cessation of this ignorance and a belief in identity.

The *Mimánsá-sutras* are the work of Jaimini, who is perhaps the same person as mentioned in the *Raghuvansa.** He is said to have been the preceptor of king Putra, the twenty-

* *Raghuvansa*, Canto 18, Sl. 33.
মহীং মহেচ্ছঃ পরিকীর্য্য সূনৌ মনীষিণে জৈমিনয়েঽর্পিতাত্মা।
তস্মাৎ সযোগাদধিগম্য যোগম্ অজন্মনেঽকল্পত জন্মভীরুঃ॥

first descendant of Ráma, the celebrated king of Ajodhyá. There was another person of that name, who is said to have been the pupil of Vyása. The *Mimánsá* is called also the *Purva-mimánsá* or *Karma-mimánsá*, as it is concerned with the *Mantras* and *Brahmanas* of the Vedas, whereas the *Vedanta* is called the *Uttara-mimánsá*, not because it is later in point of time, but because it is founded on the Upanishads, the later portion of the Vedas. The *Mimánsá* is not strictly a system of philosophy, but of ritualism; it does not investigate the nature of the soul or of matter, but reconciles the conflicting opinions of the *Srutis* and *Smritis* on ritualistic subjects. Its interpretation is given in a logical form: first is stated the *Bishaya* or the proposition which is the subject-matter of discussion, then the *Bisaya* or the doubt about it, the *Purva-paksha* or the *prima facie* wrong view of the proposition, the *Uttara-paksha* or the refutation, then the *Sangati* or reconciliation, that is, the conclusion. It has for its object the establishment of the sole authority of the Vedas. As the object of man is final emancipation from successive births, it can only be obtained by performing the ritual ceremonies prescribed in the Vedas.

The *Sánkhya* system which was founded by Kapila, was evidently set up against the doctrines of the *Vedánta.* It ignores the existence of God, repudiates the notion that anything impure can come out of pure spirit, and denies the identity of the individual soul with the universal soul. *Prakriti* or Nature is the final cause of creation; it is made up of three ingredients: goodness, passion, and darkness,* which are the causes of our happiness, misery, and affection respectively. Nature is the creator of intelligence; from intelligence comes egoism or consciousness. The latter produces the five elementary qualities, the five senses of knowledge, the five senses of action, and mind, the sense of knowledge and action; from the five elementary qualities spring the five elements; *Purusha* or soul is the last entity caused by none. Nature and the soul are eternal, and the other entities are non-eternal, being only modifications of nature just as curd and butter are of milk. Creation takes place by the union of nature and soul. The latter is different in different bodies, otherwise the happiness or sorrow of one would have affected all others: it itself does nothing, nor is it susceptible of delight and

* *Sattwa*, *Raja* and *Tama*.

pain, which belong to the intellect. It is invested with subtile and gross bodies, the latter only being liable to the three sorts of pain incident to life. As liberation is the aim, it may be effected by the annihilation of the third entity, egoism; when the conviction arises that excepting nature and soul, all other entities are nothing—mere illusions, the three sorts of pain cease, and the soul is liberated. The *Sánkhya* system is dualistic in its principle, whereas the Vedántic is non-dualistic.

The *Yoga* system is a branch of the Sánkhya: it hardly deserves the name of philosophy, being in its principle the same as the Sánkhya, with this exception that it inculcates belief in a God, and *Yoga* or meditation as the means of obtaining beatitude. Patanjali, the founder of this system, makes up the deficiency of Kapila by proving the existence of God. Everything in this world, he says, has its extremes: the climax of a minute body is an atom, and the acme of the minimum is ether; so the minimum of intelligence is gross ignorance, and its maximum is omniscience, which is never attained by man; therefore the highest intelligence is *Iswara* or God. The system of Kapila is called the atheistic Sánkhya, and that of Patanjali is called the theistic Sánkhya. Patanjali admits not only the twenty-five entities of Kapila, but adds one more, *i.e.*, God. According to his system liberation is obtained by reliance on God; reliance on God is attained by knowledge, and knowledge comes from *Yoga* or meditation. *Yoga* means union of the mind with God. It has eight limbs or stages: *Yama*, restraint; *Niyama*, religious observance; *Ásana*, posture; *Pránáyáma*, regulation of the breath; *Pratyáhára*, restraint of the senses; *Dháraná*, steadying of the mind; *Dhyána*, contemplation; *Samádhi*, profound meditation. Miraculous power is obtained by him who succeeds in meditation; he therefore easily gains the knowledge of the past, present, and future.

The system of *Nyáya* was founded by Gotama, called also Akshapáda. It is analytical as the Sánkhya is synthetical. There are sixteen categories according to Gotama. Liberation or *mukti* is effected by a knowledge of all these predicaments. The argument is this: when these predicaments are known, the knowledge of the soul arises, *i.e.*, that the soul is different from the body; consequently the illusive notion of the identification of the soul and body vanishes. When this false notion disappears, anger, envy and other passions, which are caused by this notion, disappear; the notions of virtue and vice which are the effects of these passions, never arise again. When virtue and vice disappear, which only cause new births by transmigrations of the soul, subsequent births also cease. Bodies are the sanctuaries of happiness and of misery, when therefore there are no longer births, bodies do not exist; consequently happiness or misery ceases altogether: this cessation of misery is *mukti* or emancipation.*

The sixteen categories are: 1. *pramána*, proof; 2. *prameya*, that which is to be known; 3. *sansaya*, doubt; 4. *prayojana*, motive; 5. *drishtánta*, example; 6. *siddhánta*, decision; 7. *abayaba*, parts of an argument or syllogism; 8. *tarka*, reasoning; 9. *nirnaya*, ascertainment; 10. *váda*, argument to find out truth; 11. *jalpa*, controversy; 12. *bitandá*, objections; 13. *hetwábhása*, fallacious argument; 14. *chhala*, perversion; 15. *játi*, incapacity to reply or contradictory reply; 16. *nigrahasthána*, points of defeat.

Among these *abayaba* is the most important as it contains the Hindu syllogism. It consists of five parts:

---

* Jayanáráyana Tarkapanchánana's *Sarvadarsana-sangraha.*

1. *Pratijná*, or proposition to be proved, as the hill is fiery.

2. *Hetu* or reason, for it smokes

3. *Udáharana* or example, whatever smokes is fiery as a culinary hearth.

4. *Upanaya*, or application of the reason, this hill smokes.

5. *Nigamana*, conclusion: therefore the hill is fiery.

Some of the doctrines of the Nyáya are evidently opposed to the theories of the Mimánsá: the Naiyáyikas neither attach a permanent particular meaning to any particular sound, nor do they believe in the eternity or self-existence of the Vedas, though they believe in their infallibility.

The *Vaiseshika* philosophy may be called a supplement to the Nyáya system, as it extends the investigations of the latter to physics. Kanáda, or as he is also called Uluka, was the founder of this system. He distributes his inquiries under six categories to which afterwards a seventh was added. They are: 1. *dravya*, substance; 2. *guna*, quality; 3 *karmana*, action; 4. *sámánya* or *játi*, generality or community of properties; 5. *visesha*, atomic individuality; 6.

samaváya, co-inherence or intimate relation; 7. *abháva*, non-existence or negation of existence.

The highest good is the result of the knowledge which is obtained by means of these categories. According to this system, the formation of the world is effected by the aggregation of atoms which are eternal; this aggregation and the consequent disintegration and redintegration take place by the power of *adrishta* or an unseen force. These atoms are invisible, intangible, indivisible and unperceptible to the senses. The soul is also eternal and is different from the body. Deliverance means cessation from sorrow, and is attained by means of true knowledge of the soul.

These are the doctrines of the six schools of philosophy. The works which contain the original aphorisms are certainly not voluminous, but subsequent treatises, commentaries and commentaries of commentaries, make up a large library.

We shall now notice briefly the doctrines of some of the sects which arose at a subsequent period, whose idea of obtaining deliverance from the sufferings of the world were different from those inculcated in the six systems. These doctrines, some of which are heretical and irregular, are described in the *Sarvadarsana-sangraha* of Mádhavácharya, who flourished in the fourteenth century. He was prime minister of Bukka Rai I, king of Vijayanagara, and brother of Sayana, the celebrated commentator of the *Rig-Veda.*

Chárváka was the founder of the system of philosophy which is called after his name, the *Chárváka-darsana.* Like Epicurus, he promulgated the doctrine of "eat, drink and be merry." He was materialistic to the back-bone. According to him there are only four elements: earth, air, water and fire, out of which the body is made. Though these elements are matter, yet intelligence is the outcome of this combination, as red colour arises from the combination of turmeric which is yellow and lime which is white; or as inebriating power arises from the combination of molasses and rice, which severally are not intoxicating. The soul is therefore not different from the body; hence it is mortal like the body. There is therefore no future life. Enjoyment is the only source of happiness: amusement and pleasure should be sought even by incurring debts. Tho Vedas, he says, are inconsistent in many of their doctrines, and thoy are the works of hypocrites and fools, who proscribed unnecessary pains and mortifications to the body. The Chárvákis deny any other proof except what is established by the direct testimony of our senses.

Buddhism, which is now considered a distinct religion from Hinduism, was originally a reformation of social corruptions, brought about by the restraining influence of the system of caste, the pernicious effects of ceremonial practices, and the pharisaical conduct of a selfish hierarchy. The Buddhist doctrines of deliverance and the means of obtaining it became necessarily different from those previously held. Buddha preached his doctrines in 588 B.C., more than two centuries before the invasion of Alexander, and these were reduced to writing after his death in the first Buddhist council in sets of books called the *Tripitaka.* He proclaimed that there was nothing but sorrow in life, that sorrow was produced by our affections, and that our affections should be destroyed in order to destroy the root of sorrow.* *Nirvána* or annihilation of the soul is the *summum bonum* of existence. The principles of the social and ethical codes of Buddhism, however, are more lofty and noble than those of its metaphysics.

* Max Mul'er's *Chips from a German Workshop*, Vol. I.

They proclaim the brotherhood of man, and thereby strike at the root of the system of caste. The five great negative commandments were,—not to kill, not to steal, not to commit adultery, not to lie, not to get drunk. All sorts of vice also, like hypocrisy, anger, pride, suspicion, greediness, gossiping, cruelty to animals were prohibited.* Thus Buddhism, being in consonance with the dictates of humanity, and liberal in its views and principles, became the prevailing religion of India, and it exercised at one period very great influence over the destiny of the nation. Mádhaváchárya says that the Buddhists are divided into four classes: the *Mádhyamikas* who hold that all our objects of perception are false; the *Yogácháras* who believe that the material world is unreal, the soul being only real; the *Sautrántikas* who hold that the material world is true, as is proved by inference; and the *Baibháshikas* who hold that the direct evidence of our senses proves the existence of the material world. But all these sects hold in common that proofs are of two kinds, direct and inferential; that the universe is transient, and that the body, which is com-

* Ibid.

posed of the twelve senses, must be tended with care.*

Jainaism is the only representative of Buddhism now left in India. It is said to have originated in the sixth or seventh century of the Christian era. The Jainas are divided into two sects: the *Digambaras* or those who are naked, and the *Svetámbaras* or those who are clothed in white. Those two sects, according to Mádhavácharya, are included in the general name of Árhatas, which name is, however, principally applied to the former. The Digambara Árhatas hold that separate souls exist in separate bodies, and believe in the immortality of every individual soul, inasmuch as the frequent hankering after enjoyment cannot be reconciled without a belief in the individuality and immortality of the soul. To the Svetámbara Árhatas the name of Jainas is frequently applied. They wear white dress, eat what is obtained by begging, clip their hair short, go about with a brush, and drink with their conjoined palms for fear of endangering animal life.†

According to both these sects, there are

* Mádhavácharya's *Sarvadarsana-sangraha*: *Bauddhadarsanam*: Jibánanda Vidyáságara's edition.

† *Sarvadarsana-sangraha*: *Árhatadarsanam*.

three "gems" which together effect the liberation of the soul; 1. *Samyag-darsana*, a right view or a particular care to believe in the *tattvas* of Jina; 2. *Samyag-jnána*, right knowledge or knowledge of the *tattvas* of Jina; 3. *Samyag-charitra*, right conduct which consists in the observance of the five commandments—not to kill, not to take more than what is given in charity, to speak truth, to have command over the passions, and to subdue all immoderate affections. The *tattvas* are two, five, seven, or nine, according to different sects. But the generality of the Jainas hold that there are two *tattvas:* living souls *(Jiva)* and inanimate objects *(Ajiva)*. Living souls again are divided into three classes: perfect soul, as that of Jina, liberated soul, and soul bound by worldly ties and associations.

Like the Buddhists the Jainas believe in several saints, called Jinas or Tirthankaras, who have appeared in this world for the deliverance of mankind. But it is generally believed that except the last two Jinas, Pársvanátha and Mahávira, all the others were no real personages. Pársvanátha is said to have been the founder of the sect, and Mahávira was its active propagator.

The history of Indian philosophy is involved

in obscurity; but eminent scholars have traced rationalistic speculations to the Mantra period of the Vedas. Such speculations, it seems, became common at the time of Manu. Professor Monier Williams considers that the Kshatriya class were the first to venture upon rationalism, and he quotes certain passages* from the *Chhandogya Upanishad*, from which it is plain that the Kshatriyas were the first to teach metaphysical ideas to the Bráhmanas. Buddha was of this class, being the son of Suddhodana, king of Kapilavastu. His early history shows that not only was he admitted into the principal schools of some of the important seats of learning as freely as a Bráhmana, but he himself became a great reformer and teacher of the Bráhmanas themselves. Had we been acquainted with the biographies of all the philosophers who flourished in ancient India, we should have perhaps found among them some who were not Bráhmanas; but for want of any accounts of these eminent persons, we are compelled to

* *Indian Wisdom*, p. 51. He quotes the story of Praṇahana, king of Páncháìa and Gautama *Bráhmana*. The king said "since you have sought this information (regarding the nature of the soul and future life) from me, and since this knowledge has never been imparted to any other Bráhmana before thee, therefore the right of imparting it has remained with the Kshatriyas among all the people of the world."

presume that they belonged to the first class. Bharata, who was king of India and who consequently belonged to the Kshatriya caste, was, as we have seen, the founder of dramatic literature and the inventor of some of the modes of music. Thus we see that at least up to the sixth century before the Christian era, the Bráhmanas did not monopolize to themselves all the principal branches of learning, though there was an evident tendency to confine all knowledge to their own body since the community became rganized into classes.

The eighth century of the Christian era is an important epoch in the history of the ancient Hindus. It was in this century that the great revivers of Hinduism, especially Sankaráchárya, flourished. We have already seen that Buddhism by its simple social and ethical codes which could be easily understood, and by appealing to the feelings of the nation who were hampered by the system of caste and shocked by the cruelties prescribed in the ceremonial practices, became the predominant religion of India. It became the state religion at the time of Asoka. Thus countenanced by kings and the mass of the people, it exercised dominant power from the 6th century B.C. to the 8th century A.D., and pushed Hinduism into a corner. It was a reaction—a revolt from Pantheism to Nihilism. The Bráhmanical rites were abandoned, and the Bráhmanas lost that power which they had exercised for centuries. The prevalence of the Buddhist religion for so long a period may be ascribed to its parochial system; to the monastic institutions, where education was given to the ignorant, relief to the poor, and medicines to the sick; to the itinerant life of its preachers, whose proselyting zeal was equal to any recorded in modern times; to the latitudinarian principles of the system itself; and to its tendency to exalt human nature, ignoring all philosophical distinctions between the human and the divine.

Haridwára, that hallowed spot of time-honoured memory, where the sacred Ganges first left the mountains on her way to deliver the sons of Sagara, where Daksha performed his sacrifice, and Sati became a martyr to the love of her husband, where in the eastern hill of Deváchala, Gautama passed his days in asceticism, mourning over a love shattered by infidelity,—this Haridwára was the place where the first attempt was made to revive Hinduism. Badrapádaji gave the first blow to Buddhism; he was assisted in his teachings by his disciple Nandana

Misra, and he won over a multitude of converts; indeed, he did much towards the revival of Hindu rites and ceremonies, but the final success was reserved for Sankaráchárya.* The latter preached the *Jnánakánda,* while Padmapáda, one of his disciples, preached the *Upásanákánda.* Sankaráchárya was a Drávidian: he was the celebrated commentator of some of the Upanishads and the Vedánta. He was the founder of a sect of *Sannyásis* (mendicants) called variously the Sankaráchâryas and the Dasanámi-dandinas. The *Sankaravijaya* does not mention the place of his birth, but he is said to have died at Kánchi. He travelled all over India, and his missionary tour began from Chidambara, making converts to pantheism on his way. The fanatic spirit of the people was roused; they drove away the Buddhists who were obliged to take refuge in the mountains, and in some places they were massacred by the infuriated populace.

Thus the ancient rites and ceremonies were re-introduced. Again there was a rebound, and it was from absolute nihilism to a polytheistic creed. The whole of the ancient religion was founded on the several systems of philosophy, which were based on the Vedas. The works

* *Calcutta Review*, CXVI.

that were extant on the ancient Hindu religion could with difficulty be understood even by the learned: the people had forgotten by long disuse the religious customs, and the language of the works themselves had become antiquated during the period of religious anarchy. Commentaries therefore on different religious books were written about this period to elucidate the texts, and the Puránas which were hardly read during the Buddhistic period were collected and re-introduced amongst the books to be studied.

The Puránas are called the "fifth Veda," or the Veda of the people, as they contain all rites and ceremonies which the Vedas inculcated, and settle all disputed questions on matters of religion. These works are said to have been compiled by Vyása. It appears from Manu and other writers, who flourished long before the Christian era, that some Puránas were extant before, which are now altogether lost. They were called the *Purána-Sanhitás* or *Mula-Puránas.* Vyása was the author of these *Purána-Sanhitás* in six parts which he taught his disciple Lomaharshana: the latter had six disciples, whom he taught this branch of knowledge, and these six parts were called after their names *Trarjyáruni*, *Kásyapa*, *Sávarni*,

Akritabrana Synsapáyana and *Hárita*.* These were the six old Puránas, and it is said that the other and more modern Puránas were made on the basis of these six ancient Sanhitás, three Puránas being made out of each Sanhitá by Vyása himself.

The criterion of a Purána ought to be its treatment of five different subjects : 1. *sarga*, creation of the universe ; 2. *pratisarga*, its destruction and recreation ; 3. *vansa*, genealogy of the solar, lunar and other races of kings ; 4. *manvantara*, reigns of Manus ; 5. *vansánucharita*, genealogy of celebrated beings, gods and men.† By these features the ancient works were characterized. All these Puránas expound the Sánkhya blended with the Vedánta system of philosophy. Generally speaking, all of them contain accounts of the creation, genealogies of kings and sages, legends, history, theogonies, philosophical speculations, rituals and ceremonies, also astronomy, geography, and chronology ; and in one or two works, anatomy and medicine. Thus the range of their subjects was perfectly ca-

* *Bhágavata*, XII *Skandha*, ch. 7.

† সর্গশ্চ প্রতিসর্গশ্চ বংশো মন্বন্তরাণি চ ।
বংশানুচরিতঞ্চৈব পুরাণং পঞ্চলক্ষণম্ ॥

cyclopedic. The difference which exists between them is the lead which each of them gives to some legend or other, and the substitution of one story for another.

It is evident from the eighteen Puránas* that at the time they were written, the country was distracted with sectarian discord, and it is the object of every Purána to exalt some one or other of the principal Deities. It does not, however, ignore the existence of other gods, but pays them less respect than the particular god, who is considered as the Supreme Deity. It is noteworthy that pantheism pervades or rather underlies these polytheistic notions, and they lend force to the teachings of the great Sankaráchárya.

The eighteen Upa-Puránas† were composed after the Puránas were completed, and they all possess the general characteristics of the Puránas which in relation to them are called Mahá-Puránas.

---

* The eighteen Puránas are :—*Brahma*, *Padma*, *Vishnu*, *Siva*, *Bhágavata*, *Náradiya*, *Márkandeya*, *Agni*, *Bhavishya*, *Brahma-vaivartta*, *Linga*, *Varáha*, *Skanda*, *Vámana*, *Kurma*, *Matsya*, *Garuda* and *Brahmánda*.

† The eighteen Upa-Puránas are :—*Sanatkumára Narasinha*, *Váyaviya*, *Sivadharma*, *Ascharya*, *Náradiya*, *Nandikesára*, *Ausanasa*, *Kapila*, *Varuna*, *Sámba*, *Káliká*, *Maheswara*, *Padma*, *Daiva*, *Parásara*, *Maricha* and *Bháskara*. But different writers give different names of the Upa-Puránas

The Tantras constitute a department of literature similar in character to the Puránas, but they show a still later phase of Hinduism. There are more than one hundred Tantras, and many of them were written only two hundred years ago. They constitute the fifth Veda of the Tántrikas, as the Puránas of the Pauránikas; and their authorship is ascribed to Siva, as that of the Puránas to Vyása. They are generally in the form of dialogues between Siva and Durgá, the latter inquiring into the easiest mode of deliverance from the sufferings of successive births for the benefit of the people of the Kaii Yuga, and the former instructing her in the various forms of mysticism and secret ceremonies. Most of the Tantras are based on the Sánkhya system of philosophy. The Rig-Veda says, "The Divine Spirit breathed without afflation single, with (Shwadhá) her who is sustained within him; other than him nothing existed. First Desire was formed in his mind, and that became the original productive seed;" and the Sáma Veda also speaks to the same purpose: "He felt not delight being alone. He wished another, and instantly became such. He caused his own-self to fall in twain, and thus became husband and wife. He approached her, and thus were human beings produced."* These metaphorical expressions were interpreted in a literal sense. The Prakriti of the Sánkhya philosophy was identified with Sakti, the female energy of Siva, and thus her form was worshipped as the productive seed of creation.

The original *mantra* or mystical text, according to the Mahá-Nirvána Tantra, is "The Preserver, the Destroyer and the Creator of the universe,—eternal, intelligent, one Brahma;"† this shows that the non-dualistic doctrine of the Vedánta taught by Sankaráchárya was not lost of even in this age. But this *mantra* must be sanctified by the three original *Vijas* sacred to Durgá and the five *tattvas*. The latter are the ceremonies by five objects, whose names have the letter *ma* for their initial, or the "five *makáras*" as they are called.‡ It is conceived that the performance of the rites prescribed in the Tantras gives a man

* Translated by Wilson in his *Sketch of the Religious sects of the Hindus.*

† ওঁ সচ্চিদেকং ব্রহ্ম।

‡ *Mahá-nirvána Tantra*, Bk. V., *Sls.* 22, 23.

মদ্যং মাংসং তথা মৎস্যং মুদ্রা মৈথুনমেব চ।
শক্তিপূজাবিধাবাদ্যে পঞ্চতত্ত্বং প্রকীর্ত্তিতম্॥
পঞ্চতত্ত্বং বিনা পূজা অভিচারায় কল্পতে।
শিলায়াং শস্যবাপে চ যথা নৈবাঙ্কুরোভবেৎ॥

wealth and supernatural power in this world. Among the Tantras which advocate these rites, and give minute details of their performance, the *Syámá-rahasya,* the *Devi-rahasya,* the *Rudra-yámala,* the *Kulárnava,* and the *Kámakhyá,* are the most esteemed. The *Kámakhyá Tantra* describes spells for bringing people into subjection, for making them amorous, for making them insane, for making them dumb, deaf &c., for preventing various kinds of evils ; and teaches the language of birds, beasts &c., the worship of the female energy with the adjuncts of wine, flesh-meat, women &c. Some Tantras of the Vámácháris give the ceremonies for the *Sava-sádhana,* or revivifying a corpse, for the object of acquiring command over impure spirits. The Tantras, however, denounce the rites as reprehensible if they are performed for the sole purpose of sensual gratification : and they even prescribe the quantity of wine which is to be drunk on these occasions. The practice of the ceremonies inculcated in some of the Tantras involves, indeed, sensualism of a very low type, but it must in justice be said of them that they have attempted to influence even the lowest type of men who could not be induced to perform purer ceremonies, to practice control over the mind and thereby gradually prepare them for a better and holier life. The self-control which marks out all higher types of humanity and which underlies the teachings of all these religious works for the exercise of each man's daily occupations proved too much for the Hindus of modern times. Owing partially to their surroundings and new habits, and the degeneracy due to time and nature, they ceased to follow the teachings of the sages, save only to a convenient extent consistent with one's own particular notion of duty.

We have seen that during the Mantra period of the Veda, the elements of nature were adored by the Hindus. From the similarity of the names of some of the natural forces which were worshipped by the ancient Hindus, Parsis, Greeks and Latins, it is evident that the Indo-Aryans did not migrate till nature-worship had been firmly established among the dwellers of ancient Ariana. But in the course of time rationalism began to prevail, and accordingly we find, during the Upanishad period, the Hindus deducing conclusions regarding a great First Cause from the stupendous works of creation. Monotheism became the religion of the land. But, after a long period, the growth of philosophical ideas and inquiries into the nature of God, matter and soul, the religion vacillated between non-dualism, dualism and atheism. Then came the nihilism of the Buddhists: but it is impossible for such a system to retain ascendency over the popular mind for a long time. The doctrines of the Sánkhya philosophy, which greatly influenced the minds of those who had not been converted to Buddhism, were too abstruse to be clearly understood, and accordingly we find in southern India that the Purusha and Prakriti of Kapila were worshipped in the forms of Siva and Durgá. Arrian speaks of an image of Durgá in Comorin, which he affirms was called after the name of Kumári, one of the epithets of the goddess. Image-worship therefore, if not established earlier, existed in the second century of the Christian era. While Buddhism was in full force in northern India image-worship was coming into vogue in the extreme south. But between the second and the eighth centuries, many sects arose among the Hindus who retained their ancient faith ; and at the time of Sankaráchárya we find no less than eighteen sects mentioned in the *Sankara-vijaya.* These sects must have greatly contributed to the decline of Buddhism in India.

From the second century to the eleventh century when the Vaishnava reformer Rámánuja flourished, Siva and Sakti worship prevailed in the Deccan; and then the generality of the people became converted to the Vaishnava doctrines. Madhvácharjya, called Purna-prajna in the *Sarvadarsana-sangraha*, was the founder of another sect of Vaishnavas, who made many converts to his doctrines in the Deccan. He flourished in the twelfth century. His object was to reconcile the sects of the Saivas and the Vaishnavas.* The worship of Rámachandra, the hero of the Rámáyana, was introduced into the north of India by Rámánanda in the fourteenth century, and that of Bála-Krishna by Vallabhácharya in the fifteenth century; the followers of Rámánanda are called Rámáts, and those of the latter are called Vallabhácháriyas or Mahárájás. From architectural remains in Orissa, Mr. Fergusson infers that Vaishnavism flourished before Saivaism in that province, and that Vaishnava temples existed in the seventh century of the Christian era.

The Puránas and the Upa-Puránas have greatly furthered the views of these sects, especially the worship of Brahma, Vishnu and Siva; but the worship of the first has fallen into desue-

* For the doctrines of Rámánuja and Madhvácharya, see the *Sarvadarsana Sangraha* of Mádhavácharya.

tude, and it is only in Pushkara in Rajputana that its traces continue, where a temple is dedicated to him and Sávitri, his female energy. The worship of Sakti was revived during the Tántrika period; for during the greater portion of the Pauránic times, the faith of the people was supplanted by Vaishnavism and Saivaism. The principal sects at the time of the Tantra, as at present, were the Sáktas, the worshippers of Sakti; the Saivas, the worshippers of Siva; the Vaishnavas, the followers of Vishnu; the Sauras, who adore the Sun; and the Gánapatyas, who worship Ganesa, one of the sons of Durgá.

CHAPTER V.

MANNERS AND CUSTOMS.

It is impossible to conceive that a society composed of Aryan Hindus should exist without rules of conduct to guide them in their relations to one another. The several *Smritis* or *Dharma-sástras** which contain the whole body of law consist of three *kándas* or books: *áchára* or the social customs and duties of the different castes, *vyávahára* or the practice of law and administration, and *práyaschitta* or penance. It seems that in the most ancient period Hindu society was governed by customs which, in the course of time, acquired all the force of positive law. These customary rules were at last collected and embodied in the *Grihya* and *Samayáchárika sutras* of the Vedic period. All the various works of law, which were subsequently composed, are founded upon these *sutras:* and the very words, *áchára* and *vyavahára,* which mean usages and habits respectively, convey the idea of customary laws. Among the several law-givers,† whose number

---

* *Manu*, Ch. II, *Sl.* 10—শ্রুতিস্তু বেদোবিজ্ঞেয়ো ধর্ম্মশাস্ত্রন্তু বৈ স্মৃতিঃ।

† The names of the law-givers are: Manu, Yájnavalkya, Atri, Vishnu, Hárita, Usanasas, Angiras, Yama, Apastamba,

amounts to twenty, Manu is the most ancient and authoritative. His code forms the basis of Hindu jurisprudence. It is so much revered throughout all India that it is considered as the original text, whereas the later ones are considered as expositions suiting particular localities and periods. In India the religious element enters largely in some form or other into all the systems. The Hindu jurisprudence is entirely based upon religious principles. The law of inheritance, for instance, turns upon the theory of giving funeral oblations to the deceased and succession is regulated by the nature of the spiritual benefit to be derived by the deceased from the inherent qualities of the funeral cakes. In criminal law also, leaving aside all considerations that the law-givers themselves were Bráhmans, we find that a great distinction obtains in the sanction when the offenders are either Bráhmans or Sudras, or when the offence is committed on a person of the priestly class by one of lower caste, remembering always that the Bráhmans were regarded in the light of terrestrial gods. Thus a Bráhman, guilty of all possible crimes, should not be killed, but expelled

---

Samvarta, Kátyáyana, Vrihaspati, Parásara, Vyása, Sánkha, Likhita, Daksha, Gautama, Satatapa and Vasishtha.

from the kingdom without any injury to his person, and with all his property;* a Sudra intentionally giving pain to a Bráhman should be put to death after his hands, nose or feet have been cut off.† The severity and partiality of the criminal laws of the ancient Hindus must be admitted, but they should be attributed more as sacrifice to religious principles than to their ignorance of the principles of criminal jurisprudence. So strong was this religious consideration in their mind, that we see even up to the period of the *Mahábhárata* they felt no scruple whatever in sacrificing the honour of their wives for the purpose of procreating sons, who only, in their estimation, could bestow the greatest benefit on the soul of the deceased.

In the *Institutes* there is a curious commingling of the civil and criminal codes.‡ The former is distributed under twelve heads: recovery of debts, deposits, sale of property by a person not the rightful owner, partnership, recovery of consideration money given for the performance of any particular act, non-payment of wages, breach of contract, annulment of purchase or sale, disputes between master and his herdsman,

* *Manu*, Ch. viii, *Sl.* 380.
† Ibid, Ch. ix, *Sl.* 248.
‡ *Manu*, Ch. viii, *Sls.* 4-7.

boundary-dispute, the duties of husband and wife, and the partition of ancestral property. This list does not evidently contain all the heads under which various other disputes can be distributed, but it is clear from the next stanza* that only the common and principal ones are mentioned. It will be observed from the above list that the distributions are not judiciously made, but we must freely admit that the ancient Hindus never arose above the knowledge of common principles of law. The whole of the criminal law is distributed under six heads only: assault, hurt, theft, robbery, adultery, and gambling.

The king should decide cases in person: he is advised to administer justice according to equity, custom, written codes of law and previous decisions;† if by circumstances he is unable to attend the court of justice, an educated Bráhman assisted by three others should be employed for the trial of causes;‡ persons of other castes may also be engaged, but on no account a Sudra should be employed in the administration of justice. The king is declared to be the guardian of a minor, of a barren or sonless woman not

* Ibid, *Sl.* 8.

† Ibid, *Sls.* 9, 10.

‡ *Manu*, Ch. viii, *Sls.* 3, 8, 45, 46.

maintained by her husband, and of a chaste widow.

The procedure laid down is a very simple one. The contending parties are to be heard in person, who should state their cases orally: then proofs should be adduced; all witnesses should give their evidence on oath or simple affirmation according to their rank, but no oath should be administered to a Bráhman. The judge is bound strictly to mark their demeanours. Women, on no account, are allowed to give evidence except in the case of women; and the testimony of a man who has wife and sons should be preferred, as he must be afraid of the evils which are to befall them in consequence of his giving false evidence.* Horrible denunciations are pronounced against those who give false testimony in a court of justice. At least three witnesses are necessary for establishing the facts of a case; and the code minutely lays down the classes of persons who cannot be cited as witnesses in a court of justice.

The description of a court of justice and the mode of administering justice, as it was done at the beginning of the Christian era, may be

* *Manu*, Ch. viii, *Sl.* 62.

known from the ninth act of the *Mrichchhakatika.**

The ancient Hindus had no idea of any other form of government except the monarchical. The king is said to be specially created for the protection of the people. From the period of the *Rig-Veda* the divine rights of a king are admitted: in fact he is a divinity in human shape. He is advised not to abuse this despotic power, to dispense justice without partiality, and to be devoid of avarice and other passions.

His mode of life is thus regulated by the code.† He is to rise during the last watch of the night, to perform sacrifices after purifications, to bestow alms on the Bráhmans, to enter the court for the administration of justice, to hold a council with his ministers in a solitary place, to deliberate on the affairs of the state and on the eightfold business,‡ then after performing gymnastic exercises, he is to enter

---

* *Manu*, Ch. viii, *Sls*. 64 to 67.

† Ch. vii, *Sls*. 145, 146, 216 and 221 to 225.

‡ আদানে চ বিসর্গে তথা প্রৈষনিষেধয়োঃ।
পঞ্চমে চার্থবচনে ব্যবহারস্য চেক্ষণে।
দণ্ডশুদ্ধ্যোঃ সদা যুক্তস্তেনাষ্টগতিকো নৃপঃ॥
Kalluka Bhatta's *Commentary*.

the inner apartments to dine at noon. After amusing himself for a reasonable time, and reviewing his troops and inspecting his armoury, at nightfall he is to perform the religious exercises. Then having armed himself he is to hear in a solitary chamber the reports of his spies and secret emissaries, and afterwards to re-enter the inner apartments with the ladies-in-waiting, where having recreated himself with music and taking his meals, he is to go to bed at the proper time.

That such was the course of life which the Hindu kings had followed to the time of the *Mahábhárata*, there can be no doubt at all. But the prevailing luxury of the subsequent periods introduced several alterations in the routine prescribed by Manu. Though the works of these periods are very few indeed, yet in the description of a king's life the authors must have conformed themselves to the practices of the kings of their own time. At the time of Bána, the author of the *Kádamvari,* who flourished in the seventh century of the Christian era, we find the patriarchal style of Manu had given place to a voluptuous mode of living.

A king is advised in the code to retain seven or eight ministers, but the prime minister must be an accomplished Bráhman.* Besides these, there should be ministerial officers to look after his revenue and household, a commander-in-chief and an able ambassador.

From the rules of diplomacy and war, we cannot but conclude that the whole country was divided into petty states governed by independent kings. A king is directed to consider another whose dominion is situated immediately next to his, as well as the king who favours that power, as his enemies; a kingdom situated immediately next to the inimical powers should be considered friendly, and a power beyond that as neutral.† He should bring all these powers to submission either by negotiations, presents, division, or force of arms, but negotiation is declared to be preferable to war.‡

The internal administration of the country was conducted by means of governors, who were called lords of thousand villages to whom the king delegated his powers; and they again, on their part, employed subordinate governors called lords of hundred villages. The latter again deput-

* *Manu*, Ch. vii, *Sls.* 54 and 58

† Ibid, *Sl.* 158.

‡ Ibid, *Sl.* 159.

ed their powers to lords of twenty villages, who employed lords of ten villages under them, and they again delegated their power to the lord of one village. In the whole chain, the lowest link was the ruler of a single village who was responsible to the immediate superior governor; thus every one of them was accountable to his immediate superior, till we reach the king who was responsible to none on earth. But in order to prevent all oppressions over his subjects, the king superintended the affairs of these townships, and informed himself of the administration of the vicegerents by his emissaries. From the lord of thousand villages to the ruler of one, all were remunerated by the products of the lands which the king assigned to them.

These villages referred to in the *Institutes* were undoubtedly the village communities, the traces of which might be found in all parts of India. The system was congenial to the character and convenience of the people, and inasmuch as it is contained in the much respected code of Manu, it is adhered to as any other system founded upon the national faith. This indeed accounts for its unchanging character through the successive periods of revolutions which have convulsed India since the time of Manu. "The village communities," says Lord Metcalfe,* "are little republics, having nearly every thing that they want within themselves, and almost independent of any foreign relations. They seem to last where nothing else lasts. Dynasty after daynasty tumbles down; revolution succeeds to revolution; Hindoo, Patan, Mogul, Mahratta, Sikh, English, are all masters in turn; but the village communities remain the same."

Next in importance and authority to Manu is the code of Yájnavalkya. Though its general character is the same, yet we see that some changes were introduced especially in the procedure. The allegation of the plaintiff should be taken down in writing, with his description; and the answer of the defendant is required to be given in writing.† Legal evidence is of two kinds: oral and documentary; and possession is said to raise the presumption of right.‡ Documentary evidence is to be preferred in all matters of business as it exists for a long time.§

---

* Minute of November 7th, 1830, as quoted by Mr. Phillips in the Tagore Law Lectures 1874-75, p. 7.

† Yájnavalkya, Ch. ii, *Sls.* 6, 7.

‡ Ibid, *Sl.* 22.

§ *Mahánirvána Tantra*, Bk. xi, *Sl.* 95.

লিপিঃ প্রমাণং সর্ব্বেষাং সর্ব্বত্রৈব প্রশস্যতে।
বিশেষাদ্ব্যবহারেষু ন বিনশ্যেচ্চিরং যতঃ ॥

From the most ancient times, Hindu society has been organized into classes. The caste system, however, was not quite unique in India: among the ancient Egyptians, Medes, Persians and Athenians, a similar system obtained, but we are not aware whether their kings displayed the same severity in punishing a transgressor of caste duties, as was done by Rámachandra, who cut off Sambuka's head for performing asceticism which is prohibited to a person of the Sudra class. The organisation of a society into classes cannot be an extraordinary phenomenon, it is the natural result of the different professions which its members should necessarily ply for obtaining livelihood. Society must naturally require some of its members to perform the religious ceremonies for the rest, some to govern and protect it from external aggressions, some to cultivate land for producing food-grains and supply it with the necessaries of life, and some to sell their labour to those who cannot labour themselves. This division takes place in the early stages of social life, when the arts are few and simple; but when time augments the wants of men and refinement advances, then necessarily arises an increase in the distinction of professions. That such was the case in India there cannot be any doubt: such organisation could not have been produced by the caprice of a legislator.

The Sanskrit word for caste is *varna* or colour which points to the early stage of Hindu history when India was conquered by the Aryan nation. The Aryan conquerors were fair and handsome, having come from the north, whereas the conquered aborigines, who were called *Dasyus*, were of dark complexion. In the Rig-Veda hymns, we often find that darkness of skin was a term of reproach, and applied only to the enemies of the Aryans. Thus the original distinction was that of the conqueror and the conquered,—the fair complexioned Aryans and the dark coloured Dasyus. The latter were reduced by conquest to a servile class, like the Helots of ancient Sparta, and they were afterwards called Sudras, as the Aryans were called Dvijáti,* the sacred thread being retained as the badge of the conquerors.† There is however no mention of the several classes in the earlier hymns of the Rig-Veda. Though the words *Bráhmana* and *Ríjanya* occur in them, yet they did not convey the special

* *Manu*, Ch. x, *Sl.* 4.

ব্রাহ্মণঃ ক্ষত্রিয়ো বৈশ্যস্ত্রয়ো বর্ণা দ্বিজাতয়ঃ।
চতুর্থ একজাতিস্তু শূদ্রো নাস্তি তু পঞ্চমঃ ॥

† *Manu*, Ch. ii, *Sl.* 169.

significancy which they afterwards attained; they only denoted the persons whose professions were either sacerdotal or military: any person was either a Bráhman or Kshatriya in those times according to his profession. The following stanza from the *Mahábhárata* clearly shows that the caste system was an institution of later times:—

ন বিশেষোস্তি বর্ণানাং সর্ব্বং ব্রহ্মমিদং জগৎ।
ব্রহ্মণা পূর্ব্বসৃষ্টং হি কর্ম্মণা বর্ণতাং গতং॥*

"The whole universe is Brahma, there exists no distinction of castes, because the people being created by Brahma became divided into classes according to their professions." A Sudra, says Parásara, being duly qualified, can become a Bráhman, and a Bráhman, devoid of actions prescribed to him, is not superior to a Sudra.

The earliest allusion to the fourfold division of Manu, we find in the *Purusha-Sukta*, one of the most recent hymns of the Rig-Veda:†

"From him, called Purusha, was born Viráj,
And from Viráj was Purusha produced
Whom gods and holy men made their oblation,
With Purusha as victim they performed
A sacrifice. When they divided him,

* Quoted by A. C. Datta in his *Introduction* to the *Religious Sects of the Hindus*, p. 77.

† *Mandala* x, 90.

How did they cut him up? what was his mouth?
What were his arms? and what his thighs
and feet?
The Brahman was his mouth, the kingly soldier
Was made his arms, the husbandman his thighs,
The servile Sudra issued from his feet."*

The same idea is expressed by Manu.† We need not say that these allegorical expressions were in later times taken in a literal sense; but they show at least one fact that the ancient Hindus themselves believed that these four classes instead of being derived from four different sources, were produced from one and the same individual. It is probable that the regular system of caste did not come into existence before the Yayur-Veda, but even then or at the time of Manu, the stringency of the institution had not arisen. At the time of the latter, a Sudra could marry only in a Sudra class, a Vaisya in both Sudra and Vaisya classes, a Kshatriya in Sudra, Vaisya, and Kshatriya classes, and a Bráhman in all the four classes.‡ Some of the Puráns also distinctly mention that among the three upper classes a person in ancient times

* Translated by Prof. Williams in his *Indian Wisdom*, p. 24.
† *Manu*, Ch. i, *Sl.* 31.
‡ *Manu*, Ch. iii, *Sl.* 13.

could take food dressed by one of the lowest ranks.* The fixity of a profession from generation to generation to the same families, and the strong lines of demarkation between the classes, were gradually brought about in the course of time. Manu describes also several mixed classes resulting from the intermarriage of the primary castes. Of these four primary castes, the modern Bráhmans retain their pure origin, the Rajputs are the descendants of the ancient Kshatriyas, and the Vaniyás or Vanikas of the ancient Vaisyas: but the mixed classes have greatly multiplied since the time of Manu.

Hereditary distinction is the common feature of all caste systems, but the peculiarity of the Indian institution is the religious character with which it has been invested. In order to explain the growth of the insular condition of the classes, treating each other as people of different nationality, only holding communication in those points which are distinctly laid down in the several codes, we should remember that a Hindu's sole aim of existence in this world is to secure a better one in the next. He acts, he thinks, in short, he lives not for the present but for the

---

* *Áditya* and *Agni Furáns* as quoted by A. C. Datta in his *Introduction* to the *Religious Sects of the Hindus*, p. 78.

future. The idea of transmigration, which has been propounded in the Srutis and the Smritis, forms the governing principle of all his actions. In Manu, Yájnavalkya and other Smritis, there is a chapter on *karmaphala* or consequences of acts, which gives an account of the various births which men must pass through after death according to the merits or demerits of their actions. The code of Manu describes the several classes with their respective vocations as they existed in his time, with the callings which each class could follow only in time of distress. It also contains a chapter on *karmaphala*, in which it is distinctly mentioned that a Bráhman who deviates from his rule of conduct becomes a will-o'-the-wisp* after death, a Kshatriya becomes a corpse-eating ghoul, a Vaisya becomes a filth-eating monster, and a Sudra becomes a moth-eating demon.† Now, Manu not only shows the meritorious results of the perusal of the Smritis, but enjoins the reading of his own code in a regular manner; a Bráhman reader becomes free from all sorts of sin which he may

* The *ignis-fatuus* was believed by the ancient Hindus, as is done by many at present, to have been a female-ghost which walked about in marshy places in search of prey.

† *Manu*, Ch. xii, *Sls.* 71, 72.

have committed in thought, word, or deed.* We can thus very well conceive how the laws of Manu as well as those of the other Smriti-writers were read, regarded, and acted upon, which gradually produced those strong lines of separation between the classes. Again, the duties of a class were always kept uppermost in the mind of the people by the performance of the *práyaschitta* or penances in case of violation of social duties. For any voluntary act which may lead to the loss of caste, the penance of *Santápana* is enjoined, and for an involuntary act the *Prajápatya* is to be performed.† Not to perform a penance is a sin for which a man gets an ugly life after death.‡

We cannot consider the social system of the ancient Hindus without noticing the condition of their women in former days. Though the females have from ancient times been always dependant upon the stronger sex,—a peculiarity attached to the social system of all oriental nations, yet they were treated with kindness and respect; and they possessed some rights and

* *Manu*, Ch. i, *Sls.* 103, 104.

† Ibid, Ch. xi, *Sl.* 125.

‡ Ibid, Ch. xii, *Sl.* 52. The word "ধর্ম্মস্যাসেবনেন" is explained by Kalluka Bhatta not performing penances and other meritorious acts.

freedom of which they have now been deprived. During the Vaidic period, they were considered capable of discharging the most sacred and important social duties :—a right which they possessed even at the time of the *Rámáyana* and the *Mahábhárata*. Their absolute secluded condition which has been brought on by Mahomedan oppression, has indeed much to do with the deprivation of many of their social rights. They possessed perfect liberty to be present at the sacrifices and ceremonials,* could go about in the streets in their chariots, and ascend the hall of justice for the recovery of property.† But there was an evident tendency since the time of Manu to curtail their freedom and confine them within the walls of the zenana. Manu, it appears, had no confidence in female virtue or honour.‡ She must in all stages of her life, he says, be dependant: in her childhood on her father, in her youth on her husband, and in her old age on her sons.§ She must not travel about except in the society of her husband.|| But he could not ordain their

* See the story of *Rathaviti* in the *Rig-Veda*, v, 61.
† *R. V.*, i, 166, 124.
‡ *Manu*, Ch. ix, *Sls.* 14, 15.
§ Ibid, Ch. v, *Sl.* 148 and Ch. ix, *Sl.* 3.
|| Ibid, Ch. ix, *Sl.* 13.

confinement, as he himself lays down the theory of old customs. In the *Rámáyana* also, we find that Ráma felt some scruple in being compelled to expose his wife to the gaze of the people, but excused himself on the ground that on certain occasions only women could appear in public: in great calamities, at marriage, at *Sayambara* or election of husband, at a sacrifice and in an assembly.* The literature of the subsequent period also shows that though a certain restraint was put upon their freedom, yet we see queens and highborn heroines giving audience to strangers and ambassadors, and resorting to temples and baths for purposes of worship and ablution.

But the picture we have of Hindu domestic life from ancient authors is truly charming. In spite of the social restraint put upon their liberty and of their dependant condition, Manu enjoins husbands and sons to treat women with all manner of respect and affection. In whichever family, he says, love subsists between husband and wife, prosperity increases,† and whoever seeks for fortune must supply the ladies of his household with ornaments, apparel, and food on holidays and festivals, for the curse which they bestow cwing to their ill-treatment, causes the

* *Rámáyana, Yuddhakánda.* † Ch. iii. *Sl.* 60.

ruin of the family.* A wife must always be devoted to her husband, and serve him as a god though he is devoid of all qualities, and never in thought, word or deed should dishonour him.† Women should be employed in the preservation and expenditure of wealth, in purification and domestic duties, in the cooking of daily food, and in the management of household property and furniture.‡ The picture of domestic happiness as drawn in the epics of Válmiki and Vyása, are still more beautiful and touching. Parents are fondly attached to their children, children are obedient to their parents, younger brothers love their elder brothers with all the devotedness of friends, elder brothers are affectionate to a fault, wives are loving, faithful, and obedient to their husbands, and husbands are doatingly fond of their wives. Every thing that makes the world happy and causes us to forget the troubles of life, is centred, as it were, in their descriptions, truly said to have been the effusions of inspiration, but quite natural and real. In the dramatic literature, we find that though women were not independent, yet ladies of rank received outward homage and respect; they were tended with care

* Ch. iii, *Sls.* 58 and 59.
† Ch. v, *Sls.* 154 and 165
‡ Ch. ix, *Sl.* 11.

and affection, and they possessed qualifications to make a home happy and ethereal.

There is evidence to show that in ancient India, though the women were dependant upon their male relations, yet their intellectual cultivation was not uncared for. In the most remote period we find a lady named Visvavara of the family of Atri, was the author of a hymn of the *Rig-Veda.** Her name certainly would not have been mentioned, had not education been imparted to women. In the *Brihat Áranyaka,*† Yájnavalkya is said to have taught his wife Gárgi the Veda in its difficult part, the *jnána kánda.* Manu prohibits indeed the perusal of the Vedas to women, but as his theory of domestic happiness turns upon the accomplishment and faithfulness of wives, and as he admits that a woman cannot be well secured by her male relatives by confining her within home, unless she secure herself,‡ he certainly left the other branches of knowledge open to them. Rukmini wrote a letter to Krishna expressing her love for him and her hatred for Sisupála.§ Kálidása speaks of female education in his *Kumára-sambhava* and

* *Mandala* v, hymn 18.

† Ch. iii.

‡ Ch. ix, *Sl.* 12.

§ *Bhágvat*, Ch. lii, as expounded by Sridhara Swámi.

in his dramas. Bhavabhuti mentions, Atreyi, a female devotee, as going from the hermitage of Válmiki for learning the *Vedánta* from Agastya and other sages.* Liláavati, the wife of Mandana-misra, arbitrated in the schismatic disputation of her husband and Sankaráchárjya. Later on we find in the *Mahánirvána Tantra* that a girl should be brought up and carefully instructed like a son.† All these facts leave no doubt in the mind that Hindu females were formerly educated; such noble and, we should say, unparallelled examples of faithfulness and heroism as have been recorded by ancient authors of some women, could not have been the result of ignorance: they were carefully trained and their minds properly cultivated to hold the inestimable ideas of all-sacrificing love and unflinching heroism.

There can be little doubt also that the remarriage of widows was a national custom in the Vaidic period. It can be proved by various facts. Among the *mantras* of funeral ceremonies contained in the *Rig-Veda*, which were afterwards arranged consecutively in the *Taittiriya*

---

* *Uttara Rámacharita*, Act ii.

† কন্যাপ্যেবং পালনীয়া শিক্ষণীয়াতিযত্নতঃ।
দেয়া বরায় বিদুষে ধনরত্নসমন্বিতা॥

Áranyaka of the *Black Yayur Veda*, there is one which distinctly shows that a woman could be remarried after her husband's death. According to the existing customs of those times, the wife of the deceased had to lie on the left side of the corpse on the pyre, but she was raised up by a younger brother of the deceased or a disciple or a servant with these words: "Rise up, woman, thou liest by the side of the lifeless; come to the world of the living, away from the husband, and become the wife of him who holds thy hand and is willing to marry thee."* There are also passages in the *Atharva Veda* which support polyandry, or in other words, do not denounce it as a social or religious offence, if only a trifling ceremony be performed;† *a fortiori* it may be argued that they tolerated in those times the second husband of a woman after her first husband's death. It seems however that the custom was partially abolished long before the time of

---

* Translated by Dr. Rajendralala Mitra in his *Funeral Ceremonies of the Ancient Hindus*, Journal of the Asiatic Society of Bengal, No. iv, 1870. The text is the following:

উদীর্ষ্ব নার্যভি জীবলোকমিতাসুমেতমুপশেষ এহি।
হস্তগ্রাভস্য দিধিষোস্ত্বমেতৎপত্যুর্জনিত্বমভিসম্বভূব॥

T. Aranyaka, Ch. vi.

† See Akshaya Kumara Datta's *Religious Sects of the Hindus*, p. 79.

Manu; a similar custom, which was called *niyoga*, having come into vogue at the time of king Vena. This was the permission by the deceased to a brother or any other kinsman to procreate children by his widowed wife. But Manu did not approve even of this latter custom and denounced it as sinful; he however allows a virgin girl to marry after her husband's death.* It also seems that the remarriage of widows, though reprehended, was not generally abolished even at the time of Manu, for the son of a widow by her second husband was callad *Paunarbhava*.† Válmiki, the author of the *Rámáyana*, who transferred the manners and customs of Áryávarta to the south, says that Tárá, the widow of Báli, became the wife of Sugriva after her husband's death, and Mandodari, the wife of Rávana, married Vibhishana after her husband was killed by Ráma. It is also clear from the story of Damayanti in the *Mahábhárata*, who caused a second *sayambara* to be convened for the election of a second husband, that such a custom was not considered improper, though it was not quite reputable. The *Mahánirvána Tantra* only speaks of the marriage of virgin

* Ch. ix, *Sl.* 176.
† Ch. ix, *Sl.* 175.

widows.* All these facts show that the marriage of widows was a national custom up to the period of the *Mahábhárata;* it was not abolished however till after the reign of Yudhisthira.

It was perhaps owing to the abolition of the marriage of widows in the Kali Yuga, which is said in the *Mahábhárata* to have commenced on the very day of the abdication of the throne by Yudhisthira, or shortly before, that the practice of *Sati* came into existence. It was carrying the idea of devotedness of the wife to her deceased husband to the extreme. Though not at all sanctioned by the *mantras* of the Veda, yet by an ingenious perversion of a text of the *Rig-Veda,* or by a most unfortunate mistake in its transcription, (for humanity's sake we are willing to believe the latter,) that a semblance of religious sanction was given to the rite of concremation, revolting alike to human ideas and feelings. The *mantra* we allude to is the following:—

ইমা নারীরবিধবা সুপত্নীরাঞ্জনেন সর্পিষা সম্বিশন্তাং।
অনশ্রবো অনমীবাঃ সুসেবা আরোহন্তু জনয়ো যোনিমগ্রে ॥†

"Let these women, who are not widowed, who have good husbands, apply the collyrius

* Ch. xi, *Sl.* 67.

† R. V. Mandala x, h, 18. For a detailed account, see Dr. Rajendralala Mitra's *Funeral Ceremonies of the Ancient Hindus.*

butter to their eyes; without tears, without disease, worthy of every attention, let these wives enter the house first."

We have already said that most of the *Rig-Veda mantras* regarding the funeral ceremonies were collated consecutively in the *Áranyaka* of the *Black Yayur Veda*, but without any clue to the rituals in which they should be used. Now, by a difference of reading of the text, which changed the last word অগ্রে *(first)* into অগ্নে *(of fire,)* and constructing the word *avidhavá* to mean "not to be widowed," the Hindus after the *Mahábhárata* period regarded the verse as the authority for concremation.* The real bearing of the verse as explained by Bharadvája and Baudháyana is this: on the tenth day after death the relatives by blood, both male and female, having assembled at a

---

* Raghunandana's reading is as follows:

ইমা নারীরবিধবাঃ সপত্নীরঞ্জনেন সর্পিষা সংবিশন্তু।
অনশ্বরোঽনমীব্রা সুরত্না আরোহন্তু জলযোনিমগ্নে ॥

The version of Mr. Colebrooke's is as follows:

ইমা নারীর্ অবিধবাঃ সুপত্নীর্ অঞ্জনেন সর্পিষা সংবিসন্তু বিভাবসুং।
অনসরোনারিরাঃ সুরত্না আরোহন্তু জলযোনিম্ অগ্নে ॥

which he thus translates: "Om, let these women, not to be widowed, good wives, adorned with collyrium, holding clarified butter, consign themselves to the fire. Immortal, not childless, nor husbandless, well adorned with gems, let them pass into fire, whose original is water."

place out of town, should perform a little ceremony on the fire, and the chief mourner should then repeat the verse to the women to put on collyrium, and then they should return home, the women entering the house first.* Many women on the authority of this verse alone have been burnt along with their deceased husband.

Had the authority for self-immolation been given in the Veda, Manu surely would not have left it unnoticed: he merely says that a widow should thin her body by eating holy flowers, fruits and roots: should not even take the name of a different man (with evil motive) after her husband's death, and should remain a *Brahmachárini* (religious ascetic) till her death.† The *Rámáyana* also does not mention the practice of *Sati:* the three wives of Dasaratha did not perform self-immolation after their husband's death, nor the wives of Báli and Rávana, as we have observed before. It is only in the *Mahábhárata* that the first instance of the practice occurs: Mádri burnt herself alive with her deceased husband Pándu. In the third century

* See *Funeral Ceremonies of the Ancient Hindus;* J. A. S. B., 1870, p. 256.

† Ch. v, *Sls.* 157 and 158.

before the Christian era, at the time of Alexander's invasion, the custom had become general. At the time of the *Mahánirvána Tantra,* the practice was at its height, but the author denounces it as very sinful.*

Associated with this morbid development of religious ideas, are the sacrifices of human beings who were given as offerings to the gods in ancient India. They formed the principal portion of the cultus of ancient Hindu worship. The history of this abhorrent practice may be traced to the early period of the *Rig-Veda,* in which the story of Sunahsepha establishes the fact beyond doubt.† The *Asvamedha* sacrifice, as contained in the *Taittiriya Brahmana* of the *Black Yayur Veda,* and the *Purushamedha* in the *Vájasaneyi Sanhitá* of the *White Yayur Veda,* required the immolation of human beings. But at the time of the *Satapatha Brahmana* of the *White Yayur Veda,* these sacrifices were

* Ch. x, *Sls.* 79, 80.

পঞ্চবর্ষাধিকান মর্ত্ত্যান্ দাহয়েৎ পিতৃকাননে।
ভর্ত্রা সহ কুলেশানি ন দহেৎ কুলকামিনীং॥
তব স্বরূপা রমনী জগত্যাচ্ছন্ন বিগ্রহা।
মোহাদ্ভর্ত্তুশ্চিতারোহাৎ ভবেন্নরকগামিনী॥

† See Dr. Rajendralala Mitra's *Human Sacrifices in Ancient India*; J. A. S. B., No. 1, 1876.

made typical,* and the custom of offering living human beings to the gods was not revived till after the introduction of idolatry. We have already said that the worship of *Sakti* prevailed in the second century of the Christian era. It was to this divinity that human victims were offered. Bhavabhuti, who flourished at the beginning of the 8th century, speaks in his drama of *Málati-Mádhava* of the two successive attempts made by Aghoraghantá, and his pupil Kapálakundalá, a sorceress, to offer Málati a victim to the terrible goddess Chámundá, a form of *Sakti*, but the attempts were frustrated by the timely interpositions of her friends. A detailed description of *naravali* or human sacrifice is given in the *Káliká Purána*.† Some of the *Tantras* of the *Vámácháris* advocate also this inhuman and abominable practice.

Human sacrifices in ancient India may be viewed in two different lights: first, where the victims were sacrificed by force, and secondly,

---

* Ibid.

† *Káliká Purána, Rudhiradhyaya*, See *Calcutta Review*, No. xlvii, Vol. xxiv, p. 47. "By a human sacrifice, attended by the forms laid down, Devi is pleased one thousand years, by a sacrifice of three men, one hundred thousand years, by human flesh, Kámakhyá, Chandiká, and Bhairava, who assumes my shape, are pleased one thousand years."

where they offered themselves. With regard to the former, besides the sacrifices which we have mentioned before, there was another, the custom of throwing the first born babes into the Ganges at its junction with the sea, which was observed for centuries till put down by the British government in the beginning of the present century.* The latter involved the rites of *Maháprasthána* or committing suicide by drowning one's self in the depth of the sea; *Bhrigupatana* or suicide by dashing one's self from the top of a cliff; and the *Tushánala* or burning one's self to death in a slow fire. These were the rites that were performed not only for pleasing the gods, but also for expiation and future fruition.

We shall now consider some of the habits of the people, which have at present been prohibited by the *Sástras* on the ground of utility or for warding off evil effects upon society, though enjoined before as auxiliaries for the performance of religious rites. We refer to the practices of drinking spirituous liquors and eating flesh meat, especially the bovine meat. We have already said that in the *Vaidic* period all the Hindus were addicted to the drinking of the Soma juice beer. It was a necessary article for

* *Human Sacrifices in Ancient India.*

the performance of the ceremonials and sacrifices. It is praised in the Rig-Veda: "The sound of the trickling juice is regarded as a sacred hymn. The gods drink the sacred beverage; they long for it (as it does for them:) they are nourished by it, and thrown into a joyous intoxication. Indra, the Aswins, the Maruts and Agni, all perform their great deeds under its influence. The beverage is divine; it purifies, it inspires joy, it is a water of life;......it gives health and immortality."* In short, it was considered as "a god." But the evil effects of drinking soon became known. Manu reckons the drinking of spirituous liquors to be a heinous crime—a *Mahápátaka*,† but in another place, he says that it is no crime to eat flesh meat or drink intoxicating liquors, because men are naturally inclined towards them, but desistance from such eating and drinking is of great consequence.‡ In the *Rámáyana*, though it was considered to be reprehensible, it was not absolutely prohibited. The slaying of a Bráhmana by Balaráma, and the destruction of the family of Krishna, the descendants of Yadu, are record-

* *R. V.* vi, 47. See Mrs. Manning's *Ancient and Mediæval India*, Vol. i, p. 32.

† Ch. ix, *Sl.* 55.

‡ Ch. v, *Sl.* 56.

ed in the *Mahábhárata* to have been effected under the influence of intoxication. These disastrous consequences of drinking brought on a complete prohibition. But the use of inebriating beverage at ceremonials was revived at the origination of *Sakti* worship, in which wine is advocated by the *Tantras* as a necessary auxiliary.

Flesh-meat was esteemed a valuable aliment by the ancient Hindus. Even the eating of beef, which now sounds so horrible to the ear of an orthodox Hindu, was an ordinary fact in ancient India. At the *Gomedha*, the *Sulagáva*, the *Gavamanayana*, and other sacrifices, cows were slaughtered, and the flesh distributed among the persons concerned in them.* In ancient India a cow was killed on the arrival of a guest.† Manu refers to it not only in the *Madhuparka* ceremony, but also in other usages. But the slaying of a cow is prohibited by Yájnavalkya and the *Mahánirvána Tantra* which prohibits the eating of the flesh of human beings, of animals which have the appearance of human beings, of cows which are very beneficial (to mankind) and of carnivorous animals which are

* See Dr. Rajendralala Mitra's *Beef in Ancient India*, J. A. S. B., Vol. xli.

† Bhavabhuti's *Uttara Rámacharita*, Act iv.

without any taste.* Manu gives a list, in the fifth chapter of his *Institutes*, of animals which are fit for food, among which he says "the hedge-hog, the porcupine, the guana, the rhinoceros, the tortoise are declared lawful by the wise among the five-toed animals; and all quadrupeds having one row of teeth except camels." He also declares that whoever having performed a ceremony (*sráddha, madhuparka,* &c.) in due form does not eat flesh, should after death be born an animal for twenty-one generations.† It is only since the Buddhist period, when sacrifices were abolished and when the spirit of generosity for animal life became so strong, that flesh-eating has been considered a heinous offence.

The great vice of the ancient Hindus was gambling. The consequences of gambling were as acutely felt in the early period of the *Rig-Veda,* as they were in later times. The thirty-fourth hymn of the tenth *Mandala* of the *Rig-Veda* gives a faithful picture of a gambler's life. The vice ran so high at the time of Manu that he was compelled to ordain sentence of death for

---

* *Mahánirvána Tantra*, Bk. viii, *Sl.* 108.

নরমাংসং ন ভুঞ্জীয়াৎ নরাকৃতি পশূংস্তথা।
বহুপকারকান্‌গাশ্চ মাংসাদান্‌ রসবর্জিতান্‌॥

† Ch. v, *Sl.* 35.

the offence of gambling.* Válmiki refers to it, and in the *Mahábhárata* we find that the vice had become fashionable; for Yudhisthira and Nala after losing everything they had in the world, at last staked even their wives. The *Mrichchhakatika*, a drama by king Sudraka, shows that the vice was woefully prevalent at the beginning of the Christian era.†

Some of the customs which were extant before may be known from the fact of their prohibition in the present age. We quote the following passage from the *Udváha Tatva* of Raghunandana, the author of the twenty-eight *Tatvas*, who flourished in the 16th century. The author himself quotes these passages from *Parásara, Hemádri*, the *Áditya* and the *Vrihannáradiya Puráns*. The following passages are from the *Vrihannáradiya Purána*:‡

"Sea-journey; carrying of the *Kamandalu*

---

* Ch. ix, *Sl.* 224.

† Act ii.

‡ আহ বৃহন্নারদীয়ং।
সমুদ্রযাত্রাস্বীকারঃ কমণ্ডলুবিধারণং।
দ্বিজানামসবর্ণাসু কন্যাসূপযমস্তথা॥
দেবরেণ সুতোৎপত্তির্মধুপর্কে পশোর্বধঃ।
মাংসাদানং তথা শ্রাদ্ধে বানপ্রস্থাশ্রমস্তথা॥
দত্তায়াশ্চৈব কন্যায়াঃ পুনর্দানং বরস্য চ।
দীর্ঘকালং ব্রহ্মচর্য্যং নরমেধাশ্বমেধকৌ॥

(a begging pot); marrying of girls by the twice-born classes from different castes; procreation of issues by a younger brother of the husband; slaying of animals at the *Madhuparka;* offering of flesh meat at a *Sráddha;* entering into *Vánaprastha* (or the third stage of a Bráhman's life); bestowal of girls in marriage who have already been given away (widow-marriage); *Brahmacharjya* for a long time; human sacrifice; horse-sacrifice; suicide by drowning one's self in the ocean; *gomedha* or cow-sacrifice; and sacrifices requiring immolation of cattle;—these sacrifices are declared to be prohibited in the *Kali Yuga* by the learned." *Parásara, Hemádri,* and the *Áditya Purána* prohibit in addition to these the following: "Killing of superior Bráhmans (*i.e.* those who are versed in the *Vedas*) in fair warfare even if they come to the attack;. reducing the period of mourning on account of service or for reading (the *Vedas*); performance of expiations by Bráhmans involving death; condemnation for associating with offenders; acceptance as sons other than legitimate and adopted sons; messing by a house-

---

মহাপ্রস্থানগমনং গোমেধঞ্চ তথা মখং।
ইমান্ ধর্ম্মান্ কলিযুগে বর্জ্যানাহুর্মনীষিনঃ॥

holder with a servant, cowherd, friend of the family and half-sharers (in agricultural produce) if they be of the Sudra caste; going on a distant pilgrimage; food dressed by Sudras for the Bráhmans; suicide by falling from high places or in fire; suicide on account of old age; and similar other works, are abstained from by the noble-minded and the learned lawfully at the beginning of the *Kali Yuga* for the welfare of the people: the practice of great men should be proof as strong as that of the *Vedas*."*

Notwithstanding the distinction that was made between religion and morality in some of their works, the ancient Hindus were charac-

---

* হেমাদ্রিপরাশরভাষ্যয়োরাদিত্যপুরাণং।
দীর্ঘকালং ব্রহ্মচর্য্যং ধারণঞ্চ কমণ্ডলোঃ।
দেবরেণ সুতোৎপত্তির্দত্তকন্যা প্রদীয়তে॥
কন্যানামসবর্ণানাং বিবাহশ্চ দ্বিজাতিভিঃ।
আততায়িদ্বিজাগ্র্যাণাং ধর্ম্মযুদ্ধেন হিংসনং।
বানপ্রস্থাশ্রমস্যাপি প্রবেশো বিধিচোদিতঃ॥
বৃত্তস্বাধ্যায়সাপেক্ষমঘসঙ্কোচনং তথা।
প্রায়শ্চিত্তবিধানঞ্চ বিপ্রাণাং মরণান্তিকং॥
সংসর্গদোষঃ পাপেষু মধুপর্কে পশোর্বধঃ।
দত্তৌরসেতরেষাঞ্চ পুত্রত্বেন পরিগ্রহঃ॥
শূদ্রেষু দাসগোপালকুলমিত্রার্দ্ধশীরিণাং।
ভোজ্যান্নতা গৃহস্থস্য তীর্থসেবাতিদূরতঃ॥
ব্রাহ্মণাদিষু শূদ্রস্য পক্বতাদিক্রিয়াপি চ।
ভৃগ্বগ্নিপতনৈশ্চৈব বৃদ্ধাদিমরণস্তথা॥

terized by respect to their superiors, kindness to their inferiors, faithfulness to their friends, hospitality to their guests, and gratefulness to their benefactors. Whoever, says Manu, is courteous and always serves the old, his life, learning, fame and strength increase. Never wound the feelings of a man; always give way to persons going in wheeled conveyances, to old men of more than ninety years of age, to the sick, to carriers, to women, to a Bráhman returning from his preceptor's house, to king and bridegroom: —these and other similar rules of courtesy are minutely laid down in the second and third chapters of the *Institutes* of Manu. Various moral precepts may also be gleaned from the several *Smritis*, the epics and the apologues.

ইত্যাদীন্যভিধায়

এতানি লোকগুপ্ত্যর্থং কলেরাদৌ মহাত্মভিঃ।
নিবর্ত্তিতানি কর্ম্মাণি ব্যবস্থাপূর্ব্বকং বুধৈঃ।
সময়শ্চাপি সাধুনাং প্রমাণং বেদবদ্ভবেৎ॥

CHAPTER VI.

CONCLUSION.

Thus we have briefly touched upon the arts, sciences, literature, philosophy, religion, governments, manners and customs of the Hindus, as illustrated in the *Vedas, Upanishads, Smritis, Epics, Darsanas, Kávyas, Puránas* and *Tantras*, and other works which could throw any light upon the civilization of ancient India. It is much to be regretted that the ancient Hindus did not possess any regular history, except the *Rájatarangini.* Historiography was perhaps too secular to be worthy of the consideration of a people so much imbued with religious ideas. The *Rájatarangini,* which was written by Kálhana Pandita in the middle of the twelfth century, is only the chronicle of the kings of Kashmir. But the ancient Hindus have left behind them innumerable works from which some idea of the civilization as it obtained among them, could be deduced. The several copper-plate inscriptions, inscriptions upon rocks and temples, and the various coins which are exhumed from time to time from the bowels of the earth, might also very well form a chapter of ancient

Hindu history. Like the statue, which is in the block, but which requires the laborious chiselling of the sculptor to get it out in its perfect form, the history of ancient civilization in India, which is scattered, as it were, in the monumental remains and the various works we have cited before, can only be ascertained by the laborious investigations and researches of the inquirer. Crumbling manuscripts must be looked into, and sermons should be read in brooks and stones. The works, which have been handed down to us, should be divided for the purpose of investigation, and these divisions would clearly show the several stages of development through which the Hindu intellect has passed. Thus the earliest stage is the *Sanhitá* of the *Rig-Veda;* the second the *Brahmana* and the *Aranyakas;* the third the *Kalpa-sutras* and the *Smritis;* the fourth the *Rámáyana* and the *Mahábhárata;* the fifth the *Kávyas;* and the sixth the *Puránas* and the *Tantras.* But the chronology of important events in ancient India is so very uncertain, and the biographies of the most renowned personages are such absolute voids, that we are only left to conjecture as suggested by the intrinsic evidence of their works. Thus we do not know where to place the *Darsanas*, whether before the two epics, or after or between them. It is strange that a nation who possessed so much egoism in matters of religion, should be perfectly indifferent where secular affairs are concerned.

We have already observed that one predominant idea alone swayed the course of life of the ancient Hindus. It was the idea of a future life. The doctrine of transmigration had perhaps its origin in or before the *Sanhitá* period. The march of the Hindu intellect and the consequent improvements that had taken place in the several branches of knowledge, may be proved to hinge upon this idea alone. The subsequent decline of the ancient spirit of the Hindus, and their consequent retrogression, may also be ascribed to this fact, as being brought about by the unnatural pressure of the idea put upon their intellect and genius which should have otherwise found different avenues to display and develop themselves. Their religious institution, their turn of mind, and the natural conditions of the country, were all calculated to keep up that idea in its pristine vigour. It originally shaped the national course of life and produced a healthy influence upon all the systems, but in later times its influence being not in requisition, it produced an abnormal condition of society. The shade of this idea, excluding out other influences to the institutions and systems, gave them a sickly growth and an one-sided turn. The very same influence which worked in India therefore produced different effects in the civilization of the country under the dissimilar circumstances in which it was placed: those branches of knowledge which had any connection with religion developed most rapidly, whereas others not so connected came into existence by the mere force of necessity, but either did not receive similar culture or they were neglected and forgotten.

In order to illustrate this position, we must advert to those facts which we have mentioned before. The idea of a future life which evolved into the theory of the metempsychosis underlies the religion of the Hindus in all the changes it has undergone. Man's object of life, they conceived, was *mukti* or deliverance; though they varied in their idea of it, the earliest notion, it seems, was the absorption of the soul in the essence of the Creator: till that end is attained, the soul must pass through different lives in the course of transmigration after the period of present existence. The idea of God being the concrete man whose attributes of course were magnified manifold in Him, was the common notion in the primitive states of society. The Hindus therefore were not exempted from this idea. Unless the Deity were satisfied there was no chance of escape from the miseries not only of this life but of all the existences which the soul must undergo after death. In order to pacify the omnipotent Divinity they must naturally think of giving him presents and oblations, as they would do to appease a human being when he is offended. Thus the system of sacrifices—the only form of worship known during the *Vaidic* period—was instituted, the performance of which engendered a necessity for the investigations of science, as we shall presently show.

The ideal of the Deity not differing from man in the quality of his attributes but only in degree, it was conceived that he should be pacified by getting his food, presents and oblations at the proper time. Thus night after night the ancient Hindus watched the movements of the planets and gazed upon the starry sphere to find out an auspicious moment of conjunction or opposition or entrance of the planets into some sign or constellation, when their offerings would be most complacently accepted by the Deity

Thus the science of Astronomy came into existence, and this feeling gave an impulse to the investigations of the truths of the science. To every *Veda*, therefore, a sort of astronomical treatise is appended, and however unscientific some of the calculations may appear to a reader in this enlightened age, it must be borne in mind that empiricism lies at the foundation of every science. Though we have said indeed that, according to the showing of Colebrooke, Dr. Bhau Daji, and Dr. Weber, some of the terms of Hindu astronomy have been taken from the Greeks, yet other eminent scholars do not agree with them. "Some of these, however," says Dr. Rajendralala in his *Yavanas of Sanskrit writers*, "are formed with well-known and ancient Sanskrit roots, and retain the meanings which they originally had and still have as common terms of the language, and they can no more be adduced as proofs of the Hindus having borrowed them from the Greeks, than any number of common words can be put forth as proofs of the Sanskrit language having been borrowed from the same source." Dr. Thiabaut is also of the same opinion, "for whatever is closely connected," says he, "with the ancient Indian religion must be considered as having sprung up among the

Indians themselves, unless positive evidence of the strongest kind points to a contrary conclusion."* There cannot be any doubt however that the ancient Hindus had made the science of astronomy one of their principal studies from the earliest dawn of history to the time of Bháskaráchárjya, and whatever doubt may exist regarding the borrowing of some terms by the Hindus from the Greeks, it is certain that many of their principles and observations were borrowed by the Arabs, the Chaldeans, and the Greeks themselves. The motive which gave the first impulse for the investigations of the science was indeed a powerful one; and so long as it existed, it caused considerable accession to our knowledge by the frequent observations and discoveries that were made. Such was the advancement which the science had made that even after the *Vaidic* sacrificial ceremonies had long given way to a new phase of religion, it was studied for its own sake as contributing to the elevation of the intellect, and not with a view to the propitiation of the Deity.

The discovery of the geometrical truths are also due to the sacrificial rites of the *Vaidic* period. That the origin of the geometrical

* *On the Sulvasutras*, J. A. S. B., 1875, p. 228.

science should be better understood, it must be laid down that various sorts of *vedis* or altars of different shapes and sizes were constructed by the ancient Hindus for the performance of the sacrificial ceremonies. It was conceived that the rites performed on these altars conferred different benefits on the sacrificer according to the shapes of the altars themselves. Thus the falcon-shaped altar bestowed heaven to him who performed the ceremonies on it, for he "having become a falcon himself flies up to the heavenly world;" the altar of the shape of *drona* (a measure) conferred food to the sacrificer; the wheel-shaped altar, power over enemies; thus every altar possessed peculiar inherent qualities. The construction of these altars involved geometrical operations without which the variations were not possible to be accomplished: the heights which were required to be varied at different places in the same altar; the measures which should be deduced from the general rules as of combining squares of equal or unequal sizes, turning a square into an oblong, or transforming a square into a circle; and the different layers which should contain only a certain number of bricks of different sizes and figures by a peculiar adjustment;—were certainly difficult to be managed unless previously acquainted with the principles of geometry. The rules for the size and the shape of the various *vedis*, their measurements and transformations, are given in the *Brahmanas* but the explanations of them are given in the *Sulvasutras* which are appended to all the *Kalpasutras*, the rules being expressed in the same words as in the *Brahmanas* by *Baudháyana*, *Apastamba*, and *Kátyáyana*.* Thus impelled by a religious notion to meet the requirements of the sacrificial rites, the Hindus were led to investigate the principles of geometry at so early a period as the *Brahmanas*. Long before Pythagoras discovered his well-known proposition, it had been known to the ancient Hindus; but their geometry being essentialy for practical purposes, we cannot expect to meet with the exact words of the Greek philosopher. Like the science of astronomy, the principles of geometry were investigated and improved, so long as the *Vaidic* sacrifices were considered necessary for the well-being of individuals either in this world or in the next. But in later times, we observe that the geometrical rules were employed

* For a detailed account, see the excellent work of Dr. Thiabaut *On the Sulvasutras* to which we are wholly indebted for all the information under this head.

for the purposes of astronomical calculations: the ancient Hindus must have made considerable improvements in both the sciences before they could have made geometry altogether subservient to the science of astronomy.

The origin of algebra may also be traced to the *Sulvasutras*. The necessity for the solution of indeterminate problems involved in the practical application of geometry to the erection of altars and fire-places, and also for the calculations of the motions of the heavenly bodies, first gave rise to this important branch of mathematics. The *Cuttaca*, as we have said before, was known to the Hindus long before Diophantus, and the application of the rules of algebra to astronomy and geometry was only peculiar to the ancient Hindus. There can be no doubt that the origin and the improvement of the Hindu mathematical sciences, in spite of the attempt of some writers to trace them to foreign source, may be ascribed wholly to their idea of precision in performing acts of religious duties; and that being characteristic of the people and their religion, a stricter and closer enquiry is necessary to clear up all doubts in this matter; but there is one fact which is hardly to be contested that, during the *Kalpa-sutra* period, there was scarcely a nation who had made so much advancement in mathematical learning as the Hindus had done.

The origin and scientific perfection of the grammar of the Hindus are due entirely to the same notion of pacifying the Deity. At all sacrificial ceremonies, the *Vaidic mantras* were chanted. It was conceived that the Deity would be enraged if the hymns were sung in a halting and jolting manner, or the words were wrongly pronounced, or recited without knowing their imports and bearings: not only would the sacrificer fail to attain the object of his sacrifice, but would commit a heinous sin by such wrongful recitals for which he must suffer after death. This idea indeed gave rise to the cultivation of grammar, comprising the four branches of phonetics, prosody, roots and meaning of the six *Vedángas*: *Sikshá* or the science of pronunciation, *Chhandasa* or metre; *Vyákarana* or analysis of language; *Nirukta* or exposition; *Kalpa* or sacrificial and ritual rules; and *Yotish* or astronomy. The last two do not relate to grammar. *Sikshá* or the laws of phonetics may be traced to the *Taittiriya-Aranyaka* and the *Pratisákhás* of the *Vedas*, if not earlier. The laws relating to metre or *Chhandasa* are also very old, and it is said that he who shall cause any one to repeat or shall himself repeat any hymn of the *Veda* without having acquainted himself with the metre is the "worst of sinners;" a person is said to be a *mantra-kantaka* (the destroyer of the efficacy of a *mantra)* who repeats a hymn without knowing its interpretation or the accents of the words.* These indeed were powerful incentives for the culture of Grammar at a very early period. Pánini's work is an instance of the scientific completeness of Grammar, but it should be remembered in order to account for this perfection that Panini himself mentions the names of several grammarians who preceded him. The *Niruktas* are the expositions of *Vedic* terms and phrases; many works on the subject were extant before, but the only work we have at present is that of Yáska who flourished long before Pánini.

The science of music was cultivated by the Hindus from the most ancient times, as we have observed before: its scientific culture and the perfection it afterwards attained, may also be ascribed to the same cause, that is, the sacrificial ceremonies. There are few things in the world which can enchant the human soul like music.

* Sayana's *Commentary* on the *Rig-Veda*, see *Indian Wisdom*, page 146.

However extravagant or unnatural might be the nature of the reports regarding the charming influence of the songs of an Orpheus or a Tánsen, or however still more ridiculous might be the credulity of some persons who actually believe the reports in the literal sense, yet this belief does full justice to the enchanting power of songs. Now, the conception of the Deity, as we have said, was a Being possessing all the qualities of man in the highest degree. It was considered that He would be more pleased if the prayers were sung to Him than if they were barely recited. Even to this day the notion of charming the deity by the influence of music is not uncommon in religious congregations. All the *Vaidic* hymns were therefore sung during the ceremonies. Music was consequently cultivated as a matter of necessity, the necessity for obtaining deliverance. Numerous books are extant on Hindu music, but the most ancient relating to the *Vaidic* period are either lost or to be found only by laborious researches. Though for want of chronology we cannot rank the writers according to their precedence in time, yet we are sure that the principles themselves had their origin in the *Vedic* period; the *Gándharva-Veda*, which is a branch of the *Sáma-Veda*, is the earliest work we have on the science of music, but the rules themselves must have been drawn from records existing before.

These are the Sciences which directly owe their origin to the sacrificial ceremonies of the *Vaidic* period; but Hindu philosophy was the result of speculation on the religion itself. The nature of God, His relation with man, and the mode of obtaining deliverance from the miseries of life,—in short, the rationalistic ideas may be traced to the *Upanishads* which form a portion of the *Vedas*. This was the period when the ebullition of the intellect took place,—a critical time, indeed, which shaped the intellectual march of the nation. No nation in the ancient world could vie with the Hindus in the field of philosophy and rationalistic speculations: their impressions were too deeply made upon the national mind not to show themselves at every important act of the succeeding generations. Theology and philosophy were so much blended with each other that, as it has been truly said, it is impossible to decide where one begins and the other ends. Metaphysics was not treated purely as a science of mind, but in its relation to the religion of the country. The six systems of philosophy and their commentaries display the highest flight of the intellect in the region of abstruse science, and prove the genius of the Hindus in matters where their religion is concerned. But it must be observed that they all proceed from certain assumptions, the principal of which is the eternity of the soul, and its transmigrations through successive bodies enjoying or suffering on account of the merits or demerits of the actions of a previous existence. These doctrines were so widely known,—not only by the action of the followers of the different schools, but also by the religious performances enjoined on all classes of people for throwing off the miseries of life, and likewise by subsequent writers embodying the theories in their own works,—that they were blended, as it were, with the thoughts of the people and became the motive power of their actions.

Architecture does not indeed owe its origin to the Hindu religion, but to necessity, yet the improvements in the art are wholly due to the former. Among the four *Upa-Vedas,** the *Sthápatya-Veda* relates to the science of architecture, and we have already seen that at the

* The four *Upa-Vedas* are: *Áyur-Veda* or the science of medicine, *Gándharva Veda* or the science of music, *Dhanur-Veda* or the science of archery, and the *Sthápatya Veda* or the science of architecture.

time of Manu the Hindus had made great advancement in the architectural art: the *Rámá yana* and the *Mahábhárata* also notice the improvements that were subsequently introduced; but it was not till idolatry had substituted the old religion of the country that their ingenuity in the art was called into action. Idolatry is always connected with pomp and grandeur, faith in the gods is generally displayed by splendid decorations of the temples and shrines. Mouldings, carvings, sculptures, and ornamentations were therefore resorted to, to produce what is called a striking effect. The rock-cut temples of southern India, and the remains of the shrines in Rajputana, Orissa and other places, some of which are more than one thousand years old, are still admired by foreigners for the beautiful works they contain

Thus the sciences of astronomy, geometry, algebra, grammar, music, philosophy and architecture, which attained the highest improvement, were connected with the religion of ancient India; but the other branches of knowledge, not so connected, did not receive similar attention from the people: it is necessity that led to their cultivation, and their improvement varied according to the necessity. The minds of the

Hindus were so much tinctured with religious ideas that it is not too much to say that their secular writings were very inconsiderable compared to theological works. During the thousands of years which have elapsed since the *Vaidic* period, we have only a few writers of celebrity who devoted themselves exclusively to secular subjects. Jurisprudence was not treated as a science, but it is only to meet the requirements of society that they framed those laws which are neither characterized by depth of principle nor profundity of thought: but even in this branch, a distinction is observed in the treatment of the subjects according as they were connected with religion: thus we have more works on the law of inheritance, which, as we have shown, depends on a religious principle, than on criminal laws. Trade, manufacture and the industrial arts, though their existence may be traced to the early period of the *Rig-Veda*, and though the highest success has been achieved in some of them, were, in later times, not carried on by the Hindus with that spirit or energy which they had displayed before when no social or commercial restrictions existed. Before the *Smriti* period, when the rules of caste had not matured into a regular system, commerce and manufacture were not confined to a certain class of the people, but they were carried on by the three upper classes, who were then called *Dvijátis.* We have already observed that the ancient Hindus carried on trade with various countries by sea and land, but it seems that a considerable restriction was imposed on it when sea-voyages were prohibited at the beginning of the *Kaliyuga*, that is after the period of the *Mahábhárata.* The cultivation of the science of medicine is a necessity with man, and it would subsist with his existence. Hindu medical practice has been traced to the *Rig-Veda* period, and since that time, the experiences of the Hindus have been recorded. Every attention was paid to the science: though unconnected with religion, as the necessity was strong and continuous. The extraordinary improvements which it made in India cannot be the subject of wonder, for the discovery of the hygienic properties of matter and the diagnosis of diseases were characteristic of the intelligence of the people, and the time during which the observations were made is the longest recorded of any nation. It attained its highest glory during the Buddhist period, when by the decrees of Asoka state hospitals were opened at all the principal towns and places in India for the treatment of men and animals. Subsequent Buddhist kings also kept up these institutions, and there can be no doubt that most of the celebrated medical works were written during this period. The *Atreya-Sanhitá* is said to be the oldest existing treatise on medicine, and the *Áyur-Veda* or the science of medicine is regarded by some as belonging to the *Atharva Veda*, and by others to the *Rig-Veda*.

We therefore find the combination of three circumstances which led to the development of civilization in India: (1) Religion, (2) necessity, and (3) the diffusion of knowledge which was the result of the first two circumstances among the general mass of the people. The first gave an impetus to the cultivation of the sciences, the second to the cultivation of those arts which have reference to the existence and prosperity of society and individuals, and the third relates to the promulgation of the knowledge thus obtained among the twice-born classes.

Clerical power and influence have always acted beneficially in the primitive states of society, but when knowledge increases they, instead of forwarding the movement of the intellect, become stumbling-blocks in the path of real progress.* That such was the case in India is proved by the various circumstances which led to the deterioration of the intellect, and which were brought about solely by clerical influences. From the happy beginning of the *Vaidic* period, we were led to expect a healthy movement of the intellect,—the true basis of civilization, but instead of that, Hindu society presents us with an abnormal condition after the *Mahábhárata* period, though some of the germs of it were sown long before.

In the *Vaidic* period when the people were not yet divided into regular classes; when the particular vocations which were afterwards assigned to certain classes could be carried on by any person belonging to the Aryan Hindus; when that morbid sentiment (which became afterwards more marked and strong) did not deter the clergy from messing with a trader; when a person of a certain rank could marry in a sphere higher than his own, a degree of freedom, unity and patriotism prevailed which can never be realized in the present state of Hindu society. Though the caste system could not have been the result of the caprice of any influential in-

* See Buckle's *History of Civilization in England*, Volume II, Page 4. (New Edition.)

dividual or the despotic legislation of a government, however confident it might have been on the submission and loyalty of its subjects, yet we have already seen how it was brought about by the lapse of time from the description which Manu has given of the community in his Institutes. The name of Manu acted as a charm in the minds of the ancient Hindus: he was regarded as an authority next only to the *Vedas.* That the caste system was the effect of Bráhmanical influence, however unintentionally it was exerted, must remain an undoubted fact. Down to the period of the *Mahábhárata,* however, much of the strictness of the system had not come into operation, for even then we find that intermarriage was not placed thoroughly under the ban. After the maturity of the system, when all intercourse was stopped between the several classes except what was effected by a common religion and government, the whole community had that sort of connection only which we can conceive of pebbles of certain colours placed in one and the same bag. This state of society produces the disseverance of that communion of feeling which is the basis of national strength; men become intensely selfish, and the spirit of liberty and patriotism becomes weakened under the circumstances. As a consequence of this we find the Hindus love much more their own families than their country, whereas in those places where national bond is the strongest, domestic life does not present us with that charming picture which we have in India.*

Another result of the system of caste is the monopoly of learning by the clergy. So long as war and trade were not the special professions of the Kshatriyas and the Vaisyas, knowledge was disseminated among the greater portion of the people. We have already stated that rationalism was set afoot by a person of the Kshatriya class, for Srutaketu, son of a Bráhman named Gautama, learnt it first from Pravahana, king of Pánchála, as is mentioned in the *Chhandogya Upanishad.* To the time of the *Rámáyana,* it was the bounden duty of the twice-born classes to receive education, the acquirement of which in later times became the exclusive privilege of the Bráhmans only, but at the time of the *Mahábhárata,* we find that receiving of liberal

* "In proportion," says Professor Williams, "to the weakness or rather total absence of the *national* is the strength of the *family* bond. In England and America, where national life is the strongest children are less respectful to their parents." *Indian Wisdom,* page 433, note 3.

education was considered optional with the Kshatriyas, whereas politics and the art of archery were learnt as the only duties enjoined upon them. We have already said that Sákya Sinha, a Kshatriya, studied in some of the principal seats of learning, and became the teacher of some Bráhmans before he attained his Buddhahood, but all the persons of his class did not receive liberal education like himself. The Bráhmans, it seems, were all along aware that intellect and wealth were the two powerful sources of influence in society and the superiority which the former possessed over the latter, they therefore gradually confined learning to their own body; and though ostensibly they gave up every profession that had for its object the acquirement of wealth, yet by their cleverness they managed to have all the power which wealth affords. All the superior offices under Government were in their hands, the king's principal advisers in politics and administration belonged to the clerical order, and the sacred character with which they had invested their own persons, acted powerfully on the weakness and superstition of the people, who paid ready and instant attention to the requirements of a Bráhman to avoid his curse.

Another circumstance which led to the deterioration of the intellect was caused by the Government not improving those opportunities which should have accelerated the progress of the nation. We have already said that the Hindu government was monarchical, but it was monarchical in name, whereas, in fact, it was oligarchical, and that in its worst form—that of a priestly hierarchy. Though the king was invested with the highest powers, and a sacredness which made his person inviolable, responsible to no being on earth, yet all these powers he got from the clergy to serve their interest more than that of the subjects he ruled over. In short, he was a mere puppet in the hands of the clergy, the Bráhmans ruled through him. There were indeed kings who had the courage to throw off the shackles put upon them, yet they had not the courage to introduce reforms. Any innovation that was introduced either by the people or the kings, not sanctioned by the Bráhmans, was a heresy. In the generality of instances the kings had nothing to do, except to leave the reins of government into the hands of his priestly advisers, and enjoy the luxury which the enormous wealth of the country could afford. It was therefore the interest of the Bráhmans to rule the kingdom through the ignorance and superstition of the people and the weakness of the king, and to keep up these failings as much as they could. Since learning became confined to the priestly class, it was no part of the business of the governing body to dissipate this ignorance by the introduction of liberal education among the people. We do not assert this of India before the period of the *Mahábhárata*, but there can be no doubt that such was its subsequent condition as is testified by many writers who flourished after that period.

Buddhism also, whatever credit may be due to its object of relieving the nation from the thraldom of the priesthood, contributed its mite to deaden the intellect of the nation, and thereby retarded the progress of civilization. During the long period of clerical oppression which followed the termination of the reign of Yudhishthira, when superstition had taken a deep root in the mind of the people, when sound principles of morality had given way to religious formalities, when the rules of caste were strictly enforced to convince the mass of the people of their distance from the heaven-born class of Bráhmans, not a single person had the boldness to utter a thought which was in contravention of the adopted notions of the time. The over-stretched string broke at last. Buddha was the first to proclaim the equality of man and the inefficiency of religious mortifications and ceremonials to give deliverance after death. The people flocked to him, inasmuch as his principles declared to them that they were not in any respect inferior to the so-called nobles of the land, and the kings attached themselves to his law, because it recognized their supremacy and saved them from the interference of the clergy in their dealings with their subjects. Being a Kshatriya, a prince, a highly educated man, a philosopher; and being humble, unselfish, patriotic and sincere, he was every way fitted to become the leader of the nation. Original Buddhism was nihilistic; and according to Mr. Rhys Davids, it not only anticipated Comte in his doctrines of materialism and agnosticism, but also in his worship of humanity and sacrifice of the individual to the race.* Buddhistic principles were, however, too high for the ignorant minds of the people; they therefore dragged down Buddhism to the level of their own comprehension, for the religion of a nation must fit itself to their intellectual progress, even if a high

* *Mahommed, Buddha and Christ* by Dods, p. 170.

philosophic religion be forced upon an ignorant people; we find that in the long run they make it suit their own simple notions and predilections.* This indeed explains the later phase which Buddhism assumed. Nihilism was originally preached by Sákya Sinha, but this being beyond the comprehension of the people, they filled their pantheon with innumerable deities, and transferred into it those superstitions which they had imbibed from Hinduism. Buddha himself was compelled to respect these superstitions, and there was the error: instead of meeting these superstitions with counter-superstitions, he ought to have dispelled them by enlightening the minds of the people with knowledge. Though Buddhism gave a high moral tone to the national character, and though it made the people generous, truthful, self-reliant, humane, temperate, charitable and self-sacrificing, yet these qualifications were not sufficient to forward the movements of civilization. The Spaniards possess these very qualities, but they have not saved them from retrogression.† On the other hand, Buddhism had a tendency to repress the mind within a limited range of ideas; it imparted no

* Buckle's *History of Civilization in England*, Vol. I, p. 255.
† Ibid, Vol. II, p. 585.

strength or energy to the thought; it led the mind to play in fanciful speculations; it made the people dreamy and contemplative and therefore unpractical and apathetic; under such circumstances the intellect becomes deadened, it cannot get free scope to flourish.* Therefore it is that Buddhism possesses the names only of a few great men; the whole history of the faith is almost a blank of intellectual progress.

The system of protecting literature and rewarding learned men, which has been so much deprecated by Buckle, was in full force in India from the beginning of the Christian era. We need not therefore expatiate on the evil effects of such a system. Suffice it to say that literature cannot thrive under the circumstances, and the sciences and other useful branches of knowledge, not receiving proper attention necessarily decline. Literary men lose that independence of spirit which they ought always to possess, by frequently ministering to the vanity of the king upon whose smile or reward they consider their success or eminence depends. From Sudraka to Lakshmana Sena the patronage of poets was a fashion: kings measured their glory according to the number of poets they supported in their courts. The whole

* *Calcutta Review*, Vol. XXXVIII, p. 296.

of India was divided into several petty states, all the princes of which strove with each other in their munificence to poets, or to emulate the glory of Vikramáditya, Bhoja or Harshavardhana. Ballala, who lived in the middle of the fourteenth century, mentions that Bhoja alone maintained more than five hundred poets in his court at Dhar.* So lavish was his expenditure that he is said to have dismissed a minister who had dared to remonstrate with him on account of his profuse liberality to poets and the state of the exchequer, and ordered that in future none of his advisers should prohibit him from such a course except on the penalty of death.† Thus the country was impoverished by these courtier-poets, and patronage checked that independence of the intellect which it would have otherwise attained. There were men indeed of true genius like Kálidása and Bhavabhuti, who would have been an honour to any country on the face of the earth; but there were twenty men to one of sterling merit, who were behind their age in thoughts and ideas. Only the names of a few of these poets have been transmitted to posterity, whereas the rest were supported by the sacrifice of public money, which circumstance served only

* *Bhoja-prabandha*, page 20. † Ibid, page 17.

to make literature reactionary, instead of progressive.

We have already said that Badrapádaji, assisted by his disciple Nandana Misra, gave the first blow to Buddhism, and did much for the revival of Hinduism by the introduction of time-honoured rites and ceremonies. He was followed by Sankaráchárya, who preached the *Jnánakánda*, while his disciple, Padmapáda preached the *Upásanákánda*. The royal patron of Sankaráchárya is said by some to have been Sudhanwá and by others Dharmapála. Other preachers arose to bring back the people to their ancient religion; and among them may be mentioned the names of Poithunusi, Yugmiparshma and Devala. Political influence was also brought to bear upon the zeal of these missionaries. Kumárila Bhatta became the chief leader of the persecution against the Buddhists: for it was at his instigation that king Sudhanwá passed that terrible decree for exterminating Buddhism from the face of India: "Let them be slain who slay not the old men among the Buddhists and the babe, from the bridge of Ráma to the snowy mountains." Kumárila was a very learned man: he commented on the work of *Savara-svámin* which is a commentary on the *Mimánsá-darsana* of Jaimini. Strengthened with civil power, he travelled about in various countries inculcating the doctrines of the *Vedas,* and succeeded in expelling the Buddhists from Malabar. From the eighth century the persecution continued. But at the latter end of the fifth century we find also that the hierarchs of the Buddhists were compelled to take refuge in China, Java, and other neighbouring countries outside of India, under the leadership of Dharma, one of the descendants of Buddha himself. From the works of foreign travellers, however, we find that Buddhism still lingered in India to the twelfth century, oppressed, outlawed and crushed.*

---

* *Calcutta Review*, Vol. XXXVIII, pages 270-71. It has been supposed by many that there is no evidence that the Buddhists were persecuted by the Hindus. There can be no doubt that Hinduism and Buddhism flourished side by side for many centuries, and the celebrated Vikramáditya II, king of Ujjaini in the sixth century, and Siláditya II, king of Kanouj in the seventh century, equally favoured both the Buddhist and the Hindu religion, showed equal respect to the Sramanas and the Bráhmanas and encouraged the poets of both the religion in their courts. But it is certain that in some places the Buddhists were persecuted by the Hindus. King Sudhanwá, who was the patron of Kumárila Bhatta, the great enemy of the Buddhists, and who flourished in the first half of the eighth century, that is before Sankaráchárya, promulgated an order of general massacre of the Buddhists :

আসেতোরাতুষারাদ্রে বৌদ্ধানাং বৃদ্ধবালকান্ ।
ন হন্তি যঃ স হন্তব্যো ভৃত্যানিত্যন্বশান্নৃপঃ ॥

(Mádhaváchárya).

The zeal which actuated the Hindu religionists of this period for the extermination of Buddhism, led them also to take every measure to fix the people to their ancient religion. Times had changed since Buddha preached against the ancient faith: the literary language of India had become antiquated, the people could not understand the religion; rites and ceremonials were abandoned; no distinction existed between the clergy and the laity; liberty and equality became the popular cry; and the powers which the Bráhmans had wielded before were now entirely lost. In order to regain that former influence and to prevent a relapse to a faith like that of Buddha, the Bráhmans now began from time to time to issue those books which form a considerable body of Hindu literature known by the names of *Purána*s and *Tantras*, under the authoritative names of Vyása

---

The *Brihat-Dharma Purán* (*Uttara Khanda*, Ch. 19) also alludes to the disputes between the Hindus and the Buddhists For the persecution of the Buddhists and the appropriation of Buddhist places of worship by the Hindus, see *Asiatic Researches*, Vol. XV, p. 264, Hunter's *Orissa*, Vol. I, Ch. V, and Dr. R. Mitra's *Orissa*, Vol. II, p. 58. There is therefore sufficient evidence to show that the Buddhists were ruthlessly persecuted and massacred by the Hindus from the 5th to the 8th century of the Christian era. It appears, however, that finally Buddha and most of his tenets were gradually absorbed into the Hindu religion, Buddha being accepted as one of the nine *Avatars* (incarnations) of Vishnu.

and Siva. Ostensibly these works professed to expound the ancient Hindu religion, whereas they were intended to check every act, every notion and every idea of the people, so that they might not go astray from the path chalked out for them by the Bráhmans. The intellect was shackled: the people were thrown into the vortex of superstition. The freedom of thought was lost: it was environed on all sides with superstition. The people learned in order to be ignorant. This was the crowning circumstance which brought the civilization of the country to a stand. What was effected by the other circumstances was slow and gradual, but now the finishing stroke was given. Buddhism, in spite of all its faults, was a thousand times better than the resuscitated faith: it did not check the freedom of the intellect, though it gave it a wrong and fanciful turn; and what became of the nation afterwards for want of this freedom of the intellect, we leave the reader to infer from the pages of authentic history.

The condition of the people before the period of the *Mahábhárata* was certainly not so abject as it became after that period. The clergy were well aware that to secure their own influence they must propitiate the people and thus gradually bring about a thorough submission. Therefore was it ordained that the king should always love and protect his subjects as his own children,* and should always have their welfare at heart. The generality of the people were educated like the Bráhmans, the Sudras being left to learn by filtration from their own masters whom they served. The first question which Ráma asked Bharata when they met in the forest was, whether the subjects were happy and in the enjoyment of prosperity. Yudhisthira was also very popular because he acted according to the rules laid down for kings. When Bráhmanical influence had not yet become predominant, the princes considered it their paramount duty to seek the welfare of their subjects and their prosperity. The voice of the people carried much weight with them, and they uttered it without fear or favour. Ráma exiled his wife in submission to the people, because they wanted that she should pass through an ordeal to prove her chastity. But after the period of the *Mahábhárata*, we find that the kings became luxurious, the Bráhmans were supreme in the kingdom, and held the reins of government. It is only as an exception and not as a rule that

* *Manu*, Ch. VII, *Sls.* 135, 139.

we see a truly bold and wise monarch on the throne. Vikramáditya, disguising himself like Haroun-al-Raschid or Akbar, travelled about in the kingdom to learn the grievances of the people with his own ears. Bhartrihari is said to have killed his own favourite wife, because she might endanger the safety of the kingdom by revealing what is called a state-secret. Imbued with strong imagination from the natural conditions of the country, steeped in superstition, the people were now afraid to utter that voice which had been law unto kings before. There would certainly have arisen a different civilization in the country, had the sciences which were inaugurated by the *Vaidic* rites been allowed to grow in an independent manner, but the increase of clerical influence impeded the genius of the people, which after the *Kalpa-Sutra* period arrived at a point when the interference of the clergy became a clog to the march of the intellect. Though we have seen that between the fourth and the seventh centuries, an impetus was given to the cultivation of science, yet for want of historical records we are unable to alight upon the true cause, but it seems that this movement was intended for reviving the ancient *Vaidic* ceremonies which had been forgotten by the people during the prevalence of the Buddhist faith. But it is certain that such knowledge did not become general, only a few Bráhmans kept up scientific pursuits in their obscure schools even down to the seventeenth century, as we have already seen in the reluctance of the authors of the *Súrya-Siddhánta* and *Siddhánta Siromani* to publish their discoveries and inventions. After the period of the *Mahábhárata*, especially when Buddhism lost its former influence, the people only talked of religion, heard of religion and met religion everywhere. Freedom of thought they lost, and dared not broach any opinion lest it should clash with the adopted notions of the time. They gave themselves up to credulity and superstition, renounced their proper duties, and regarded themselves as passive instruments to serve the will of the clergy.

We have laid much stress on the clerical influence having contributed to the deterioration of the Hindu intellect. It should, however, be observed that this was due to the decline of learning amongst the clerical body after the *Mahábhárata* period, and as a consequence wrong and perverted interpretation was given to the *Shástras* with a view to selfish and interested motive. The *Shástras* and other books for the regulation of conduct, it must be confessed, contain many liberal texts and principles which are wide enough to give a free scope and play to the Hindu intellect. Besides the clergy, the other classes likewise contributed their mite to the downfall of the nation. They also did not cultivate those particular sciences, arts and professions which by natural law, in course of time, became stereotyped to each particular caste.

Thus we see that the abnormal state of Hindu civilization is the effect of circumstances which have been working from a very remote period. One circumstance indeed could not have produced such a state of society; the civilization which grew up in the *Vaidic* period was healthy, vigorous, and progressive, but it got a misdirected turn by the combination of all the circumstances which we have stated before. The consequences brought about by a single circumstance were added to those of others which followed. Hindu civilization has left its foot-prints on the rock of the past, engraven—never to be effaced, both in its forward and backward movements; both of these are worthy of the observation and consideration of sociologists, as signs of health and symptoms of disease. The circumstances which we have before mentioned in detail, may be briefly enumerated as follows: (1) the system of caste, (2) confinement of learning to one particular class, (3) withholding by government of opportunities of national progress, (4) Buddhism in its connection with the national intellect, (5) patronage of poets, (6) the influence of the *Purânas* and the *Tantras* in generating superstition, and (7) the abject condition of the people.

The whole history of the civilization in ancient India proves that the Hindu intellect passed through three periods:—

1. The theological and practical,
2. The philosophical and speculative,
3. The superstitious and ignorant.

The present state of our knowledge regarding ancient India warrants us in drawing the conclusions we have already arrived at, but when by further researches other facts will be brought to light, they will elucidate many points in the history of the Hindu intellect which we at present do not understand. There is at present an indication of revival of learning: the publication of original Sanskrit works with commentaries and interpretations has now been commenced, which will no doubt not only help to awaken the Hindu intellect but also serve to disperse many of the mistaken notions now entertained on many points in the history of civilization of ancient India.

FINIS.